DEPARTMENT OF THE NAVY
HEADQUARTERS UNITED STATES MARINE CORPS
2 NAVY ANNEX
WASHINGTON, DC 20380-1775

MCO P10120.28G
LPC
8 Jul 05

I0415837

MARINE CORPS ORDER P10120.28G

From: Commandant of the Marine Corps
To: Distribution List

Subj: INDIVIDUAL CLOTHING REGULATIONS (SHORT TITLE: ICR)

Ref: (a) DoD 7000.14R, Volume 7A (DoDFMR), "Military Pay
            Policy and Procedures-Active Duty and Reserve Pay"
        (b) DoDI 1338.18, "Armed Forces Clothing Monetary
            Allowance Procedures"
        (c) MCBul 10120, "Fiscal Year (FY) Individual Clothing
            Allowances"
        (d) MCO P1020.34G, "Marine Corps Uniform Regulations"
        (e) MCO 10120.31F, "Introduction of New C&T Items Into
            the Department of Defense (DoD) Supply System"
        (f) United States Code, Title 37, "Pay and Allowances
            of the Uniformed Services"
        (g) MCO P1080.40C, "Marine Corps Total Force System
            Personnel Reporting Instruction Users Manual (Short
            Title: MCTFSPRIUM)"
        (h) MCO P1070.12K, "Marine Corps Individual Records
            Administration Manual (Short Title: IRAM)"
        (i) TM-10120-15/1, "Technical Manual for Uniform
            Fitting and Alteration"
        (j) MCO 10120.61, "Dress Blue Uniforms Presented to
            Recruit Honor Graduates"
        (k) MCRCO 10120.2, "Blue Dress Uniform Issue to Delayed
            Entry Program Members with Three Enlistment
            Referral Credits"
        (l) SECNAVINST 1640.9B, "Department of the Navy
            Corrections Manual"
        (m) NAVSO P-1000, "Financial Management Policy Manual"
        (n) MCO P3040.4E, "Marine Corps Casualty Procedures
            Manual (Short Title: MARCORCASPROCMAN)"
        (o) NAVMEDCOM 5360.1, "Decedent Affairs Manual"
        (p) JAGINST 5890.1 "Administrative Processing and
            Consideration of Claims on Behalf of and Against
            the United States"

**DISTRIBUTION STATEMENT A: Approved for public release;
distribution is unlimited.**

(q) MCO P7301.104, "Accounting Under the
    Appropriations 'Military Personnel, Marine Corps'
    and 'Reserve Personnel, Marine Corps'"

(r) DRAFT MCBul 7301, "Fiscal Year (FY) Accounting Under
    the Appropriations Military Personnel Marine Corps
    (MPMC) and Reserve Personnel Marine Corps (RPMC)"

(s) MCO P4050.38C, "Personal Effects and Baggage
    Manual"

(t) TM 4700-15/1H, "Ground Equipment Record Procedures"

(u) MCO 4855.10B, "Product Quality Deficiency Report"

(v) MCO 4400.137A, "Defense Logistics Agency Regulation
    DLAR 4235.18"

(w) United States Code, Title 10, "Armed Forces"

(x) MCO P11000.12C, "Real Property Facilities Manual,
    Volume II, Facilities Planning and
    Programming"

(y) MCO P11000.5F, "Real Property Facilities Manual,
    Volume IV"

(z) MCO P1700.27A, "Marine Corps Community Services
    Policy Manual (Short Title: MCCS Policy Manual)"

(aa) DLAI 4140.55, "Reporting of Supply Discrepancies"

(bb) UM 4400-15, "Organic Property Control"

(cc) MCO P4400.150E, "Consumer-Level Supply Policy Manual"

(dd) MCO P3000.19, "USMC Total Force Mobilization,
     Activation, Integration, and Deactivation Plan
     (Short Title: USMC MAID-P)"

Encl: (1) LOCATOR SHEET

1. <u>Situation</u>. To publish Marine Corps policy on the
administration of individual uniform clothing and clothing
allowances.

2. <u>Cancellation</u>. MCO P10120.28F, MCO 10120.56B, chapter 6 of
MCO P4400.151B, and the Memorandum of Understanding (MOU), dated
10 Oct 00, between the Deputy Commandant for Installations and
Logistics (DC, I&L) and the Deputy Commandant for Manpower and
Reserve Affairs (DC, M&RA) for Operation and Management of Marine
Corps Military Clothing Sales Store (MCSS) Facilities.

3. Mission. Commanders will take action as necessary to disseminate the information contained herein and to administer ICR per this Manual.

4. Execution.

    a. Commander's Intent and Concept of Operations

        (1) Commander's Intent. To ensure that individual uniform clothing and clothing allowances are appropriately administered and provided to authorized personnel, per references (a) and (b).

        (2) Concept of Operations. This Manual should be used in conjunction with individual clothing allowances published annually in reference (c), and other current regulations and directives to ensure compliance with policies and procedures outlined in this Manual.

    b. Subordinate Element Missions. Refer to chapter 1 of this Manual.

    c. Coordinating Instructions. This revision contains a complete rewrite of the ICR and incorporates policy previously published in the Logistics Support of Marine Corps Uniform Clothing and Textile (C&T) Programs (MCO 10120.56B); and, therefore, should be reviewed in its entirety.

5. Administration and Logistics

    a. The currency, accuracy, and completeness of this Manual and its distribution are the responsibility of CMC (LPC).

    b. The maintenance and upkeep of this Manual are the command's responsibility.

    c. Recommendations concerning the contents of this Manual are invited and should be forwarded to the Commandant of the Marine Corps (LPC) via the appropriate chain of command.

6. <u>Command and Signal</u>

    a. <u>Signal</u>. Effective the date signed.

    b. <u>Command</u>. Applicable to the Marine Corps Total Force.

RICHARD L. KELLY
Deputy Commandant
Installations and Logistics

DISTRIBUTION: PCN 10210880000

    Copy to: 7000050, 7000260, 172 (2)
              7000153 (10)
              7000110 (2)
              7000144/8145001 (1)

LOCATOR SHEET

Subj: <u>INDIVIDUAL CLOTHING REGULATIONS (ICR)</u>

Location: _____
          (Indicate the location(s) of the copy(ies) of this
          Manual.)

INDIVIDUAL CLOTHING REGULATIONS

RECORD OF CHANGES

Log completed change action as indicated.

Change Number	Date of Change	Date Received	Date Entered	Signature of Person Entering Change

INDIVIDUAL CLOTHING REGULATIONS

CONTENTS

INDIVIDUAL CLOTHING REGULATIONS

INTRODUCTION

0001. <u>PURPOSE</u>. This Manual provides policy and procedural guidance for the administration of individual clothing and accessories and clothing allowances.

0002. <u>RELATIONSHIP TO OTHER REGULATIONS</u>

1. This Manual includes policy guidance and instructions for the administration of individual clothing and clothing allowances. Detailed procedures contained in this Manual are limited to those related to individual clothing that are not contained in other Marine Corps directives.

2. <u>Related publications</u> are as follows:

   a. <u>Fiscal Year (FY) Individual Clothing Allowances (MCBul 10120)</u>. This Bulletin, published annually, provides a listing of all Marine Corps clothing allowances, to include initial clothing allowances, supplementary clothing allowances, and cash clothing allowances that are funded by Military Personnel, Marine Corps (MILPERS) appropriations. This Bulletin also provides the Minimum Requirements Lists (MRLs) showing the items individuals are required to possess.

   b. <u>Product Quality Deficiency Report (MCO 4855.10B)</u>. This Order provides instructions for preparing, submitting, and processing product quality deficiency reports (PQDRs).

   c. <u>Introduction of New Clothing and Textile (C&T) Items Into the Department of Defense (DoD) Supply System (MCO 10120.31F)</u>. This Order provides instructions for submitting supply request packages for new clothing items and proper procedures for developing clothing phase-in/phase-out plans.

   d. <u>Technical Manual for Uniform Fitting and Alteration (TM-10120-15/1)</u>. This Manual provides instructions for size selections and fitting for uniform clothing items.

   e. <u>Marine Corps Uniform Regulations (MCO P1020.34G)</u>. The Marine Corps Uniform Regulations provide policy and guidance concerning the authorized manner in which uniform clothing items will be worn.

f. Marine Corps Total Force System Personnel Reporting Instruction Users Manual (Short Title: MCTFSPRIUM)(MCO P1080.40C). The MCTFSPRIUM provides detailed reporting information on the entitlement of clothing allowances.

g. Department of Defense (DoD) Financial Management Regulation (FMR)(DoD 7000.14-R, Volume 7A). The DoD FMR provides overarching Armed Forces policy on the administration of clothing allowances.

h. Accounting Under the Appropriations "Military Personnel, Marine Corps" and "Reserve Personnel, Marine Corps" (MCO P7301.104 W CH 1-9) w/Ch 1-9. This Manual provides detailed accounting data to be used in accounting for obligations and expenditures for clothing allowance issues and other clothing transactions. MCBul 7301 will be published to provide updated appropriation data and fiscal instructions for managing clothing allowance issues.

i. Personal Effects and Baggage Manual (MCO P4050.38C). This Manual provides instructions for the administration and disposition of personal effects and baggage when personnel become separated from their effects.

j. Defense Logistics Agency Regulation DLAR 4235.18 (designated as MCO 4400.137A). This Regulation provides policy and procedures for the requisitioning and supply of special measurement clothing and footwear and orthopedic footwear.

k. Armed Forces Clothing Monetary Allowance Procedures (DoDI 1338.18). This Instruction provides policy and procedures for the administration of Armed Forces clothing monetary allowances.

l. Consumer-Level Supply Policy Manual (MCO P4400.150E W Erratum and Ch 1-2). This Manual provides supply policies for use in the effective control of equipment and materiel processed through Marine Corps consumer-level supply organizations.

m. USMC Total Force Mobilization, Activation, Integration, and Deactivation Plan (USMC MAID-P) (MCO P3000.19). This Manual provides policy for the clothing and equipping of Marine Corps Reserves and other personnel during contingency operations.

3. The Reserve Establishment will continue to supplement the instructions contained in this Manual with Reserve-specific directives, as required.

0003. ACRONYMS. Acronyms and other abbreviations used within this Manual are contained in appendix A.

INDIVIDUAL CLOTHING REGULATIONS

CHAPTER 1

ROLES AND RESPONSIBILITIES

INDIVIDUAL CLOTHING REGULATIONS

CHAPTER 1

ROLES AND RESPONSIBILITIES

1000. INTRODUCTION. Administration of individual clothing and clothing allowances requires a coordinated team effort by several clothing stakeholders. Clothing allowances, in particular, are unique, in that they cross boundaries between supply and manpower entitlements and are not incorporated within the Expeditionary Force Develop System. The Commandant of the Marine Corps (CMC) is the approving authority for all uniform clothing allowances and allowance changes. The Permanent Marine Corps Uniform Board (PMCUB) makes clothing allowance recommendations to CMC and seeks additional funding, with the support of Subject Matter Experts (SMEs) from various organizations (detailed below).

1001. SCOPE. Clothing stakeholders and their primary roles and responsibilities are identified in figure 1-1 following. This chapter provides detailed roles and responsibilities for the administration of individual clothing.

1002. COMMANDERS. Unit and organization commanders are responsible for enforcing the policy contained within this Manual. First and foremost is the responsibility to protect the spirit and intent of the clothing allowances to ensure no unauthorized issues are charged against the Military Personnel Marine Corps (MILPERS) and Reserve MILPERS open allotments for clothing allowances. Specific clothing responsibilities are as follows:

1. Ensure strict compliance with this Manual when authorizing individual clothing allowances, ensuring that allowance issue forms are accurately and completely filled out and reflect the actual allowance items and quantities authorized, per chapter 3 of this Manual.

2. Ensure completion of required clothing inventories, per chapter 3 of this Manual.

3. Perform clothing inspections to ensure serviceability, proper fit, and compliance with applicable Minimum Requirements Lists (MRLs), per chapter 4 of this Manual.

4. Collect clothing upon separation of specific individuals and provide disposition of recovered clothing, per chapter 6 of this Manual.

5. For those commands operating a Retail Clothing Outlet (RCO), provide oversight for RCO functions and ensure those responsibilities detailed in paragraph 1008 following are accomplished.

1003. DEPUTY COMMANDANT, INSTALLATIONS AND LOGISTICS (DC, I&L). DC, I&L is responsible for publishing USMC clothing administration policy in compliance with overarching DoD policy and providing technical support and guidance to the Permanent Marine Corps Uniform Board (PMCUB). Specific clothing responsibilities are as follows:

1. Establish clothing program logistics support responsibilities and policy for the administration of individual clothing and equipment.

2. Work with the PMCUB to develop uniform and accessory project directives, as required, for both system and non-system clothing items.

3. Assist the PMCUB with the development of an annual budget for uniform clothing initiatives and clothing allowances.

4. Provide clothing allowance rate information to assist the PMCUB with allowance decisions and implementation plans and to assist CG, MARCORSYSCOM with new clothing fielding plans.

5. Coordinate annual Marine Corps Clothing Allowances and CRA with the Department of Defense (DoD).

6. Publish annually, per fiscal year (FY), all applicable clothing allowances and MRLs.

7. Provide policy oversight and assist with supply support to Military Clothing Sales Stores (MCSSs) and RCOs, to include:

    a. Coordinate with Defense Supply Center, Philadelphia (DSCP) on clothing item pricing.

    b. Provide timely notification and guidance to all clothing stakeholders concerning policy changes.

    c. Provide technical assistance on uniforms and uniform matters as required.

    d. Provide policy oversight to the administration of agreements between the Marine Corps and the Army and Air Force Exchange Service (AAFES) and the Naval Exchange Command (NEXCOM) for sale and/or issue of uniform clothing.

1004. <u>PERMANENT MARINE CORPS UNIFORM BOARD (PMCUB)</u>. The PMCUB is the program sponsor for uniform clothing, accessories, and materials and is responsible for execution of CMC authorized clothing allowances and uniform wear regulations. <u>Specific clothing responsibilities of the PMCUB are as follows</u>:

1. Consider any matter related to Marine Corps uniforms in which a perceived problem exists or in which a possible improvement can be made, via a seabag review or similar reviews. Implement new clothing allowances or clothing allowance changes, as necessary. The basic process for implementing new or modified clothing allowances is outlined in figure 1-2 following. A need for a new clothing allowance (either via cash payment or in-kind issue) or an allowance change is presented to the PMCUB for consideration. The PMCUB uses research and development (R&D), allowance working groups, and technical support and guidance from clothing SMEs to consider the requests, analyze fiscal impact and supportability, and make recommendations to the formal MCUB. The formal MCUB is a task-organized board facilitated by the PMCUB to address new or modified allowance recommendations. The formal MCUB then makes recommendations to the Commandant of the Marine Corps (CMC), via the Assistant Commandant of the Marine Corps (ACMC) Committee. The ACMC Committee comments on the MCUB's recommendations and forwards to CMC for decision.

2. Initiate new clothing item project directives (to improve existing items or develop new items) in order to:

    a. Develop and/or fabricate proposed uniforms, materials, and accessories.

    b. Introduce approved items into the Federal supply system or the military clothing sales system (Marine Corps Community Services Exchange (MCX), Army and Air Force Exchange Service (AAAFES), and Navy Exchange Command (NEXCOM)).

3. Approve designs and materials for all uniform clothing and accessory items, to include field uniform items.

4. Coordinate with clothing stakeholders and SMEs to develop a budget for uniform initiatives (including R&D and new item fielding) using the Program Objective Memorandum (POM) process. Prioritize available funding for new uniform clothing fielding and new uniform clothing allowances and assist with the fielding plan for new clothing items.

5. Administer and approve all uniform clothing allowances and MRLs.

6. Approve an implementation plan for new or modified clothing allowances.

7. Establish the need for and authorized wear of uniform clothing, accessories, and materials. Uniform wear regulations are not discussed in this Manual as they are provided in reference (d).

1005. DEPUTY COMMANDANT, PROGRAM AND RESOURCES (DC, P&R). DC, P&R is responsible for providing fiscal instructions for clothing administration and oversight of the clothing budget. Specific clothing responsibilities are as follows:

1. Provide technical support and guidance to the PMCUB for development of an annual budget for uniform clothing initiatives and clothing allowances. Provide data on MILPERS and Reserve MILPERS funds available for clothing allowances to assist the PMCUB with allowance decisions and implementation plans and to assist CG, MARCORSYSCOM with new clothing fielding plans.

2. Coordinate with CG, MARCORSYSCOM for funding associated with new item fielding, to include initial item cost, applicable Clothing Replacement Allowances (CRAs) and price increases for existing allowances. Provide CG, MARCORSYSCOM, upon submission of a supply request package (SRP), the fund to be billed (i.e. appropriation data, signal code, fund code, etc.), address of billing office, and point-of-contact.

3. Provide fiscal instructions and oversee the spending of MILPERS/Reserve MILPERS for the clothing budget line. Coordinate with M&RA throughout the year if any variances occur in the budget plan.

1006. DEPUTY COMMANDANT, MANPOWER AND RESERVE AFFAIRS (DC, M&RA). DC, M&RA is responsible for the administration of MILPERS appropriations and operation of MCX MCSSs. Specific clothing responsibilities are as follows:

1. Provide the PMCUB with technical support and guidance, including manpower plans and data, planned accessions and numbers of personnel in allowance rating billets. This data will assist with clothing allowance decisions and allowance fielding and implementation plans.

2. Provide fiscal programming and budgeting oversight, via the POM officer, for all clothing allowances to include initial clothing allowances, supplementary clothing allowances, cash clothing allowances, and miscellaneous and special issues.

3. Provide MILPERS POM programmatics (formats, timelines, etc.) and assist the PMCUB with submission of the POM and related initiatives (Unfunded Programs List, Unified Legislation and Budgeting initiatives, Budget Estimate Submission, etc.) for clothing allowances.

4. Provide issues and sales of supply system uniform clothing items and sales of commercial non-system uniform clothing items via MCX MCSSs. Provide for uniform clothing alterations, per paragraph 2009.2 of this Manual.

5. Provide for deployment support of uniform clothing items via MCX MCSSs. Ensure that MCSS mobilization plans parallel and support HQMC

operational plans concerning the disposition of Marine Corps MCSS stocks in the event of mobilization. See paragraph 9003 of this Manual.

6. Provide oversight to the MCX MCSSs per chapter 5 of this Manual and ensure compliance with all applicable Marine Corps policies and procedures.

7. Prepare procurement instructions and invitations for quotations and administer contracts for the procurement of approved non-system uniform clothing items.

8. Consolidate requirements and establish stockage points/objectives for system and non-system uniform clothing items provided for sale and/or issue at MCX MCSSs.

9. Develop and provide CG, MARCORSYSCOM with long-range uniform sales projections for the purpose of budgeting and planning basic uniform material requirements.

10. Coordinate with CG, MARCORSYSCOM and CG, MARCORLOGCOM to ensure that:

    a. Contractors meet and maintain quality control standards. In this regard, DC, M&RA will coordinate with all MCX MCSSs in the submission of QDRs for non-system items and Product Quality Deficiency Reports (PQDRs) for system items, per paragraph 5004 of this Manual.

    b. Uniform clothing specifications or commercial item descriptions (CIDs) and patterns are current.

11. Provide representation at DSCP reviews of materiel obligations (backorder briefs).

12. Provide for disposition of recovered clothing, to include recovered clothing sales, per chapter 6 of this Manual.

13. Respond to requests from other HQMC organizations for management/operational information in response to audits, Congressional inquiries, etc.

1007. COMMANDING GENERAL, MARINE CORPS LOGISTICS COMMAND (CG, MARCORLOGCOM). CG, MARCORLOGCOM is responsible for uniform clothing distribution and item management and management of Navy Working Capital Funds (NWCFs) for the operation of military clothing sales stores (MCSSs) and retail clothing outlets (RCOs). Specific clothing responsibilities are as follows:

1. Act as the Secondary Inventory Control Activity (SICA) for the Marine Corps to help resolve specific uniform clothing supply support problems, as identified.

2. Provide information for data calls, integrated product teams, etc., regarding sustainment and availability of uniform clothing items.

3. Provide Marine Corps liaison to DSCP in order to interface between item managers and USMC customers and to resolve issues on uniform clothing requisitions.

4. Manage the PQDR Program for system uniform clothing items and perform quality control/quality defect resolution visits to various USMC sites.

5. Coordinate, host, and conduct customer support conferences and site visits, to include DSCP reviews of materiel obligations (backorder briefs), inviting, at a minimum, representatives from I&L, M&RA, the PMCUB, MARCORSYSCOM, the MCSSs (Marine Corps, NEXCOM, and AAFES), and the Retail Clothing Outlets (RCOs).

6. Serve as designated focal point to process clothing related Catalog Action Requests (forms DD 1277), forwarded by CG, MARCORSYSCOM.

7. Research information and provide usage data to Marine Corps activities.

8. Serve as screening point monitor for Marine Corps Supply Discrepancy Reports (SDRs).

9. Manage requests for disposition of excess clothing items, to include redistribution and disposal.

10. In coordination with the CG, MARCORSYSCOM, maintain sufficient quantities of all Marine Corps optional officer materials as protected stocks to ensure availability of subsequent sale to approved contractors/individuals, until exhausted.

11. Oversee the Memorandum of Agreement (MOA) between the Marine Corps and AAFES for operation of MCSSs in Okinawa.

12. Oversee and pay fees associated with the MOA between the Marine Corps and the NEXCOM for providing mail order support services for uniform clothing items to Marine Corps personnel worldwide. This MOA is executed by the Commanding General, Marine Corps Logistics Bases (MARCORLOGBASES).

13. Manage and fund the NWCF used on loan to M&RA Marine Corps Community Services Exchange (MCX) and AAFES (on Okinawa) to stock MCSSs. Per paragraph 3003 of this Manual, CG, MARCORLOGCOM will increase the money value of the initial loan, as required, so that the MCSSs can maintain sufficient stock to support each installation's requirements.

1008. COMMANDING GENERAL, MARINE CORPS SYSTEMS COMMAND (CG, MARCORSYSCOM). CG, MARCORSYSCOM is responsible for total life-cycle program management of uniform clothing items. Specific clothing responsibilities are as follows:

1. Provide supply and logistics support and requirements/demand determination for system and non-system uniform clothing items.

2. Provide technical support and guidance to the PMCUB in order to develop a budget for uniform clothing R&D and quality assurance activities. Coordinate with the PMCUB for development of a POM and budget for new uniform clothing fielding, associated CRAs, price increases for existing allowance items, and sustainment.

3. Perform uniform clothing R&D and new item development, as directed by the PMCUB via uniform project directives.

    a. For new items, fabricate or procure a minimum of nine samples for each item; seven to be maintained by MARCORSYSCOM, one for PMCUB and one for the Marine Corps Historical Center, Building 58, Washington Navy Yard, Washington, DC 20374 (Attn: Registrar).

    b. For each item introduced into the Federal supply system or for an item currently in the system that has changed significantly, CG, MARCORSYSCOM shall tag six of the sample items as guide samples and provide them to DSCP for use in procurement.

4. Perform clothing design functions for the Marine Corps by developing and maintaining detailed drawings and current specifications/CIDs, preparing patterns, fabricating and/or procuring prototypes, experimental fabrics, and items/accessories, as directed or required.

5. Provide DC, P&R, in writing, the total projected price quotation and subsequent up-front funding changes for new item introduction.

6. Coordinate item standardization review, including substitutability/acceptability, and supply planning data for federal supply system items. Specifically:

    a. Coordinate with DSCP on projected up-front funding costs in support of new system item introduction/standardization and provide DC, P&R in writing the total projected price quote. Any subsequent up-front funding changes will also be provided to DC, P&R.

    b. Initiate, prepare, and submit Catalog Action Requests (forms DD 1277) for newly introduced items and SRPs, requirements data, etc., to DSCP, per reference (e), via CG, MARCORLOGCOM. Include in the SRP the fund to be billed, address of billing office, and point-of-contact.

    c. Develop phase-in/phase-out plans, per reference (e). Coordinate with DSCP, DC, I&L, DC, P&R, DC, M&RA, CG, MARCORLOGCOM and the PMCUB on all proposed phase-in/phase-out plans. Provide timely notification and guidance to all clothing stakeholders concerning disposition of phase-out merchandise to allow sufficient and appropriate actions.

7. Initiate and evaluate technical or manufacturing changes in specifications/CIDs for existing Marine Corps uniform items and

materials when such changes will result in ease of manufacturing or higher percentage of acceptability of finished items, without in any way altering the appearance or basic utility of the improved item. Proposed specification/CID changes that will alter the appearance, basic utility, or basic fabric of an item will require prior approval of CMC via the PMCUB. Provide subject approved changes to the Institute of Heraldry.

8. Establish shade tolerance and approve/disapprove shade deviations based upon evaluation and recommendations of the DSCP laboratory for system uniform clothing items, where neither the appearance nor the function of the item is affected.

9. Provide quality assurance for all uniform clothing items as follows:

    a. Establish and maintain a Marine Corps Uniform Items Certification Database of approved commercial sources of supply for non-system uniform clothing items authorized for sale through the military clothing sales system. This area of responsibility includes soliciting, receiving, inspecting, and approving/disapproving samples of uniform clothing and accessories from manufacturers and distributors.

    b. Upon acceptance of the manufactured sample, issue an approval number/USMC serial number and letter of approval to the manufacturer/distributor. One tagged sample will be returned to the manufacturer/distributor, and one tagged sample will be maintained for reference purposes. Furnish DC, M&RA, DC, I&L, and the PMCUB a copy of each letter of approval.

    c. Maintain liaison with approved commercial sources and the MCSSs/RCOs to ensure that the quality of Marine Corps uniform items supplied meet Marine Corps standards and specifications/CIDs. Perform, as required or requested, onsite visits to suppliers for first article inspections and follow-up visits, as necessary.

    d. Resolve quality deficiency reports received for non-system uniform clothing items. Remove from the approved source listing those suppliers that do not correct reported deficiencies or continue to provide items not meeting Marine Corps standards. Cancel approval numbers for items discontinued by individual

suppliers. Prior to canceling uniform approval numbers,
coordinate with DC, M&RA and provide DC, M&RA, DC, I&L, and the
PMCUB a copy of each cancellation letter.

    e. Establish and maintain liaison with CG, MARCORLOGCOM and
DSCP, as required, to ensure that the quality of Marine Corps
uniform clothing items and materials supplied through the federal
supply system meets Marine Corps standards and/or
specifications/CIDs. Ensure that DSCP expeditiously resolves
PQDRs for system uniform clothing.

10. Provide newly established approved sources with
specifications/CIDs and a full range of patterns on a one-time
basis free of charge when awarded a contract. Subsequent expense
for replacement patterns or pieces shall be borne by the approved
source. Approved sources that have not been actively producing
but were previously provided a full range of patterns will only
be provided revised pattern pieces/revisions free of charge, to
include specification/CID changes/revisions.

11. Provide, as requested, detailed specifications/CIDs and a
standard size pattern, including all changes thereto, to DC,
M&RA, AAFES, and/or NEXCOM, for use in competitive procurement
for those non-system uniform clothing items provided through the
military clothing sales system.

12. Coordinate and assist, as required, DC, M&RA in the
preparation of invitations for quotations for the procurement of
approved Marine Corps officer optional uniform items.

13. Attend meetings for clothing and textile (C&T)
standardization projects with other military services and
industry. Present and defend the Marine Corps position based on
R&D and evaluation studies for items under discussion within the
guidelines of Marine Corps policy and established procedures.

14. Provide representation at DSCP reviews of materiel
obligations (backorder briefs). Subsequent to each meeting,
provide a status-type report to DC, I&L, DC, M&RA, and via
MARADMIN (when required) within 10 working days.

15. Publish new item availability and initial fielding message
notification and limited availability messages, as required, in
coordination with CG, MARCORLOGCOM.

16. Provide assistance to field activities regarding supply support problems pertaining to Marine Corps uniform clothing items.

17. Coordinate with Marine Corps Logistics Base Albany to maintain sufficient quantities of all Marine Corps optional officer materials at the direct support stock control activity to ensure availability of subsequent sale to approved contractors/individuals, until exhausted.

18. Provide useful service life data on all new system uniform items and periodically perform research to adjust existing useful service life data, as the useful service life is a critical component for establishing the CRA.

1009. RETAIL CLOTHING OUTLETS (RCOs). There are only two remaining RCOs in the Marine Corps; RCO Quantico, VA and RCO San Diego, CA. The primary function of the RCO is to support Initial Clothing Allowance issues to candidates at the Officer Candidates School (OCS), Quantico, VA and recruits at Marine Corps Recruit Depot (MCRD), San Diego, CA. RCOs may also provide for sales, issues, and deployment support of authorized supply system uniform clothing items to other organizations, if sufficient stocks are available, per the policy in this Manual. Specific clothing responsibilities are as follows:

1. Consolidate requirements and establish sufficient stockage points/objectives for system uniform clothing items provided for issue.

2. Develop and provide CG, MARCORSYSCOM with long-range uniform issue projections for the purpose of budgeting and planning basic uniform material requirements.

3. Provide representation at DSCP reviews of materiel obligations (backorder briefs).

4. Provide for uniform clothing alterations, per paragraph 2009.2 of this Manual.

5. Perform fiscal accounting, per chapter 3 of this Manual.

6. Perform those source of supply responsibilities detailed in chapter 5 of this Manual.

7. Provide for the disposition of recovered clothing, per paragraph 6004 of this Manual.

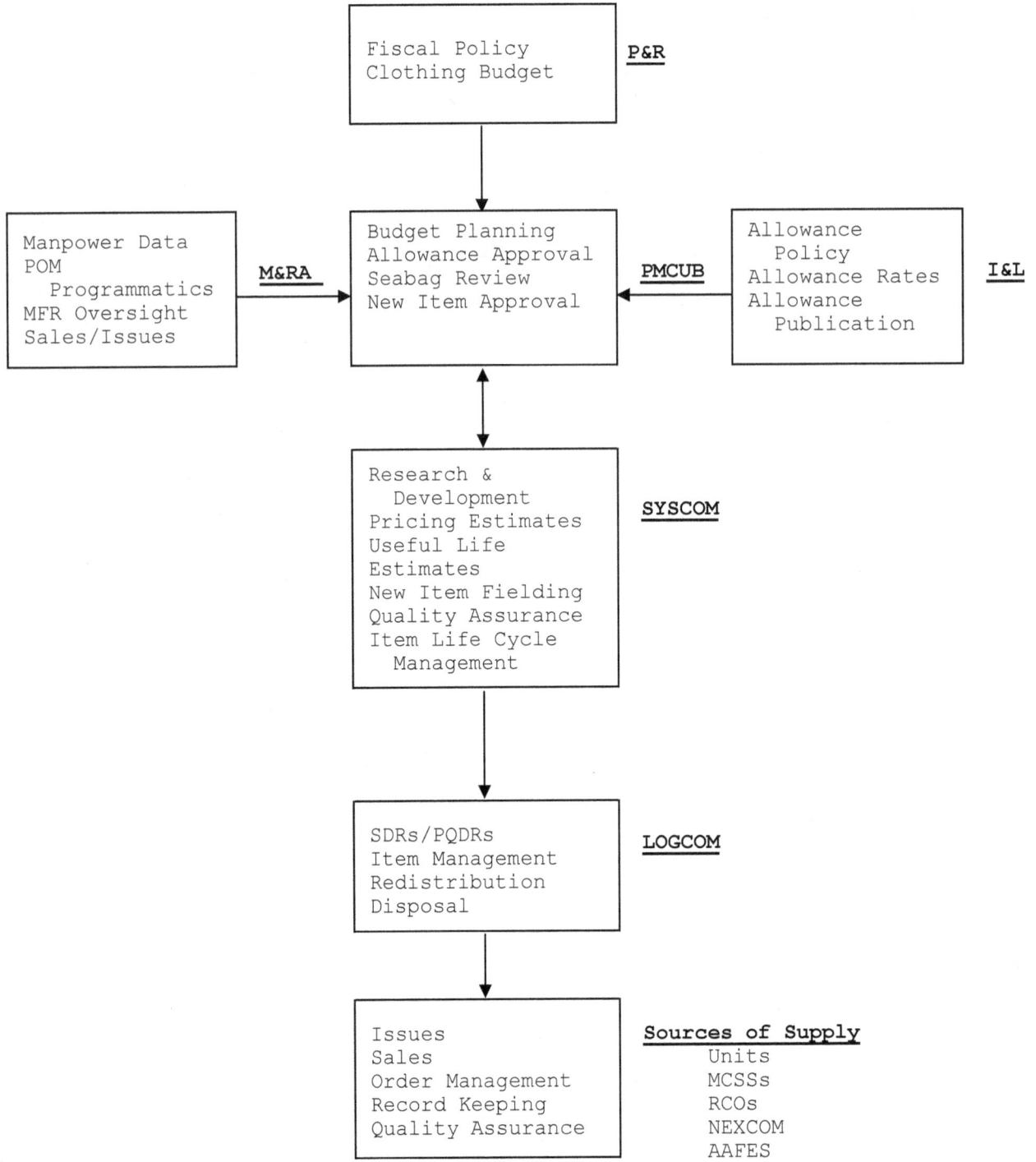

Figure 1-1.—Clothing Allowance Stakeholder Roles and Responsibilities.

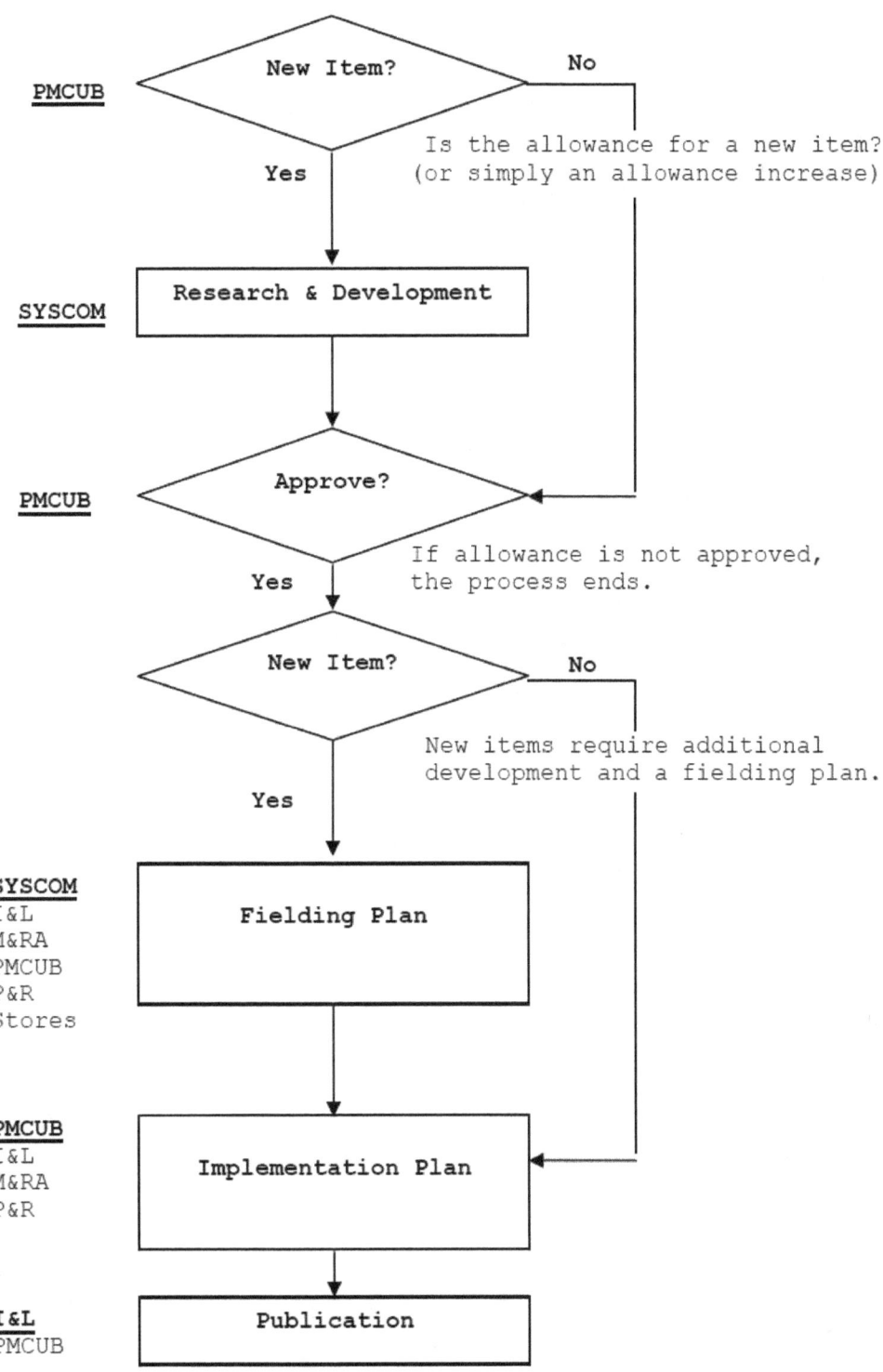

Figure 1-2.—Clothing Allowance Implementation.

INDIVIDUAL CLOTHING REGULATIONS

CHAPTER 2

CLOTHING ALLOWANCES AND OTHER CLOTHING ISSUES

INDIVIDUAL CLOTHING REGULATIONS

CHAPTER 2

CLOTHING ALLOWANCES AND OTHER CLOTHING ISSUES

2000. <u>INTRODUCTION</u>. Reference (f) directs the services to provide enlisted service members with all uniforms required for wear. Initially, this requirement is met by issuing all recruits the Initial Clothing Allowance (commonly known as the "sea bag") at recruit training. Marine recruits are issued required uniforms, t-shirts, shorts, and sweat suits; free of charge. This chapter contains a listing of the Initial Clothing Allowance (seabag) issue and other authorized clothing allowances, issues, and entitlement criteria. Allowances are gratuitous, i.e. at government expense. Authorized personnel do not pay for allowances, neither directly nor via pay checkage. Specific items, quantities, and/or cash payments to be issued for these authorized allowances are published annually, at the beginning of each Fiscal Year (FY), in reference (c). Recruits are charged for required personal items (running shoes, personal hygiene items, etc.) and services (haircuts and laundry) during boot camp, as these are not funded by the Government. Officers are required to provide their own individual uniform clothing. The furnishing of individual clothing to officers on other than a sales basis is not authorized, except as otherwise specified in this Manual or as directed by the Commandant of the Marine Corps (CMC).

2001. <u>SCOPE</u>. These allowances pertain to enlisted personnel of the Regular and Reserve Establishment (unless otherwise specified), Reserve personnel on extended active duty (more than 6 months of active duty), and authorized civilians serving with the Marine Corps, as designated. Reference (c), published annually, contains amplified instructions for new or modified allowances and, where in conflict, takes precedence over the policy contained herein. Additional allowances and procedures for Reserve personnel are provided in chapter 8 of this Manual.

2002. <u>TYPES OF AUTHORIZED ALLOWANCES</u>. Uniform clothing allowances are authorized under the DoD Clothing Monetary Allowance (CMA) System, per the DoDFMR. Allowances can be provided as either clothing gratuitously issued or as cash paid to authorized individuals. Clothing issued under the CMA System may not be replaced in-kind (one-for-one replacement), unless specifically authorized in writing by HQMC. Clothing items issued to personnel under the provisions of these allowances may be either new or serviceable recovered clothing suitable for resale, per paragraph 6004 of this Manual. Serviceable recovered clothing will be the first source of supply considered for allowance issues. Initial Clothing Allowance issues may be either new or condition code A, per paragraph 6004 of this Manual, at the commander's discretion. All of the allowances described in sections 2003-2008 are funded by Headquarters Marine Corps managed Military Personnel, Marine Corps (MILPERS) and Reserve MILPERS appropriations. Those other issues and services described in paragraph 2009 are funded as specified. Authorized allowance issues and services consist of the following:

- Initial Clothing Allowances
- Special Initial Clothing Allowances to Navy Personnel
- Initial Clothing Allowances for Officer Programs
- Clothing Replacement Allowances (CRAs)
- Cash Clothing Allowances
- Supplementary Clothing Allowances
- Other Clothing Issues and Services

2003. INITIAL CLOTHING ALLOWANCES. Initial clothing allowances in this section are only authorized for enlisted personnel and only one entitlement to an initial clothing allowance will accrue during any period of continuous active duty in an enlisted status. Initial clothing allowances consist of:

1. Initial Issue to Recruits, Reenlistees, or Activated Personnel (seabag issue). This Initial Issue is authorized under the following instances:

    a. Upon first enlistment or induction in the Marine Corps (both Regular and Reserve).

    b. Upon reenlistment in the Regular Marine Corps, acceptance of an Active Reserve contract, or assignment to extended active duty (more than 6 months of active duty), subsequent to expiration of 3 months from completion of Marine Corps obligated service (i.e., must have been off of obligated service for 90 days or more). See chapter 9 of this Manual for additional details on issues to reservists recalled to active duty during partial or total mobilization/activation, including issue of a Minimum Combat Load (MCL) in lieu of an entire Initial Issue.

c. Upon enlistment or reenlistment in the Marine Corps following discharge from another branch of the service.

d. Upon recall to active duty, subsequent to the expiration of 3 months from the date of last release/retirement from active duty (to include personnel of the Fleet Marine Force Reserve); also known as a "non-obligor." Only one such allowance shall be authorized during any period of 4 consecutive years. See chapter 9 following for additional details on issues to recalled retirees.

e. Upon reenlistment in the Regular Marine Corps after having been on the temporary disability retirement list in excess of 18 months.

2. <u>Initial Issue to Enlisted Musicians of the U.S. Marine Band</u>. This Initial Issue is prescribed each FY with the maximum monetary value set by the Secretary of Defense. This allowance is authorized to both male and female enlisted personnel under the following instances:

a. Upon appointment to the U.S. Marine Band.

b. Upon appointment to the U.S. Marine Band, following discharge from another branch of the service.

If appointed to the U.S. Marine Band from another band or drum and bugle corps of the Regular Establishment, the Initial Issue will be reduced by the amount of clothing they were last required to maintain, as documented on the Individual Clothing Record (NAVMC 631/631A).

3. <u>Reduced Initial Issue to Reserve Reenlistees or Activated Personnel</u>. This Reduced Initial Issue is authorized when a member has enlisted from a Reserve component of the Marine Corps (i.e., is still under obligated service, also known as an "obligor") or has been off of obligated service ("non-obligor") for less than 3 months. This Reduced Initial Issue consists of the Initial Issue reduced by the amount of clothing the

individual was last required to maintain (i.e., exit inventory per paragraph 3004 of this Manual), as documented on the NAVMC 631/631A. A MCL may be issued in lieu of an entire Initial Issue to mobilized/activated personnel, per paragraph 9002 of this Manual.

    a. For <u>Individual Ready Reservists (IRRs)</u> the Reduced Initial Issue consists of the difference between the current active duty MRL and the active duty exit inventory. Unserviceable clothing possessed by the individual and listed on the exit inventory will be replaced at government expense, only once, immediately upon reenlistment.

    b. For <u>Selected Marine Corps Reservists (SMCRs)</u> the Reduced Initial Issue consists of the difference between the current active duty MRL and the current reserve MRL. Unserviceable clothing possessed by the individual and listed on the exit inventory will be replaced at Government expense, only once immediately upon reenlistment.

4. <u>Reduced Initial Issue to Commissioned Officers or Warrant Officers</u>. This Reduced Initial Issue is authorized when an officer enlists, reenlists, or reverts to enlisted status to serve on active duty, other than for the purpose of retirement or transfer to the Fleet Marine Corps Reserve.

    a. This Reduced Initial Issue consists of the Initial Issue reduced by the items and quantities contained in the officers' minimum uniform requirements list, per reference (d).

    b. Entitlement to this Reduced Initial Issue will not be considered as the "last authorization of an initial allowance" for the purpose of determining entitlement to a CRA. Only one such allowance will be authorized during any period of 4 consecutive years. Unserviceable clothing possessed by the individual and listed on the exit inventory will be replaced at Government expense, only once immediately upon enlistment, reenlistment, or reversion.

5. <u>Reduced Initial Issue to Unsuccessful Officer Candidates</u>. This Reduced Initial Issue is authorized when the candidate is assigned to further duty in an enlisted status. This Reduced Initial Issue consists of the clothing necessary to bring the amounts furnished the individual up to the current active duty MRL.

6. Reduced Initial Issue to Enlisted Prisoners. This Reduced Initial Allowance is authorized to enlisted personnel restored to duty after being sentenced to confinement and punitive discharge. This Reduced Initial Issue consists of only the items of clothing recovered during their personal effects inventory, per paragraph 6003 of this Manual. The individual will be required to purchase those items still required after the preceding issue has been made, in order to bring the quantity of clothing in that person's possession up to the applicable MRL. Policy for issue to prisoners (while still in a prisoner status) is provided in paragraph 2009 following.

7. Issues to Civilians Serving with Marine Corps Units. Issues to civilians serving with Marine Corps units are authorized when so designated by CMC via the Permanent Marine Corps Uniform Board (PMCUB). Authorized civilians may wear Marine Corps service or utility uniforms with designated civilian technician insignia, but no distinctive grade or Marine Corps or Navy device or insignia may be worn, per reference (d). Documentation of such issues will be recorded on a Combined Individual Requisition and Issue Slip (NAVMC 604/604) and maintained by the issuing organization for record keeping purposes only. NAVMC 631/631B is not required.

2004. SPECIAL INITIAL ALLOWANCES TO NAVY PERSONNEL. Navy personnel, both Regular and Reserve, serving with Marine Corps units are authorized the following special initial clothing allowances:

1. Special Initial Utility Uniform Allowance (SIUUA). The SIUUA is intended for Navy enlisted personnel who routinely wear the utility uniform during the performance of their work while assigned to Marine Corps units.

    a. The SIUUA is authorized for Regular Navy enlisted personnel and Reserve Navy enlisted personnel on extended active duty (more than 6 months of active duty), permanently assigned or assigned on a Temporary Additional Duty (TAD) basis for augmentation purposes due to contingency operational commitments to Marine Corps forces, or on inactive duty assigned to SMCR support units.

b.   Authorized Navy enlisted personnel will receive only one entitlement to this allowance during any one period of continuous assignment to such duty. Additionally, personnel who have received this allowance will not be authorized a subsequent allowance of the same items upon assignment to a new Marine Corps unit if less than 3 years have elapsed between assignments (i.e., there must be a 3-year break in service with the Marine Corps in order to receive a new SIUUA).

c.   Navy officers may purchase and wear the utility uniform at their option and expense, per the Navy appearance standards.

2.   <u>Special Initial Service Uniform Allowance (SISUA)</u>. The SISUA is intended for Navy Hospitalmen (HMs), Dental Technicians (DTs), and Religious Persons (RPs), both Regular and Reserve on extended active duty (more than 6 months of active duty), permanently assigned to Marine Corps units (other than combat-committed units) and drilling Selected Naval Reserve personnel in these ratings on inactive duty assigned to SMCR support units. Those assigned to combat-committed units will receive the SIUUA above only.

a.   Authorized Navy enlisted personnel will be given a 60-day option period in which to elect to wear the Marine Corps service uniforms. This 60-day period begins upon the member reporting to the gaining force command (GFC). Those who elect to wear and maintain Marine Corps service uniforms will be provided the SISUA. Navy personnel who receive this allowance will be required to wear these uniforms as directed for the duration of their continuous service with a Marine Corps organization and will abide by Marine Corps uniform and grooming regulations, per reference (d). Those who elect not to wear Marine Corps service uniforms will wear their Navy service uniforms, when service uniforms are required.

b.   Navy enlisted personnel will receive only one entitlement to this allowance during any one period of continuous assignment to such duty.

c.   Navy enlisted personnel who have received this allowance will not be authorized a subsequent allowance of the same items upon assignment to a new Marine Corps unit if less than 3 years have elapsed between assignments (i.e., there must be a 3-year break in service with the Marine Corps in order to receive a new SISUA).

d. Navy officers may purchase and wear the Marine Corps service uniform at their option and expense, per the Marine Corps grooming and physical appearance standards provided in reference (d).

2005. <u>INITIAL ALLOWANCES FOR OFFICER PROGRAMS</u>. The Initial Clothing Allowance for officer programs is authorized for:

- Platoon Leaders Course (PLC) Candidates
- Officer Candidates Class (OCC) Candidates
- Naval Reserve Officers Training Corps (NROTC) Marine-Option Midshipmen
- Service academy students directed to attend Officer Candidates School (OCS), MCCDC, Quantico, VA

1. Enlisted personnel selected for assignment to a military service academy as a student, enrolled in the NROTC, or selected to attend OCS as a candidate are responsible for retaining their issued Marine Corps clothing. Accordingly, only those items and quantities of the applicable allowance which are in excess of the applicable MRL will be issued. If an individual returns to extended active duty (more than 6 months of active duty) within 3-months of last separation from active duty, the individual is considered as having been in a "continuous active duty status" and remains under the CMA System until appointment as an officer (i.e., clothing replacement in-kind is not authorized). In the event the enlisted person is discharged from a military service academy or the NROTC or fails to complete OCS, credit toward entitlement of the cash CRA will only be given for active duty with the Marine Corps.

2. Personnel who receive this Initial Clothing Allowance will not be entitled to cash CRA.

2006. <u>CLOTHING REPLACEMENT ALLOWANCE (CRA)</u>. CRA amounts are prescribed annually by the Secretary of Defense and are based on the replacement price and useful service life of items in the Initial Clothing Allowance ("seabag"). CRA is paid in cash via direct deposit to regular enlisted Marines and reserve enlisted Marines on extended active duty (more than 6 months of active duty) to replace individual seabag items, as required. CRA payments are made in addition to other pay and allowances and are paid annually, at the end of the Marine's enlistment anniversary month. Reserve enlisted Marines, not on extended active duty, are not eligible for CRA. Drilling reservists are authorized replacement in-kind of clothing items, per chapter 8 of this Manual.

1. Purpose. CRA accrues on each Initial Clothing Allowance (seabag) item monthly and is to be used with discretion by the individual for the replacement of seabag items initially issued or to purchase newly fielded seabag items (i.e., items on the MRL).

    a. Seabag MRL inspections should be conducted routinely to ensure that CRA is effectively managed. It is recommended that an individual inspection be monitored by the command concurrent with each Marine's annual CRA payment.

    b. CRA is not intended to cover the cost of repair, laundering, dry-cleaning, or alteration of clothing.

    c. Whenever feasible, improved or new individual uniform clothing items introduced will be phased in during a time period that will allow personnel to accrue CRA to purchase the new item. Concurrent with the phase-in of the new item, a fair wear-out (phase-out) period will be announced for individual uniform clothing items replaced/deleted from initial and/or supplementary allowances.

    d. Enlisted Navy personnel who are furnished Marine Corps clothing continue to receive Navy CRA while serving with Marines. Therefore, they are not entitled to CRA from the Marine Corps.

2. Types of CRA. CRA is payable in two types, basic and standard, based on the enlisted persons time on active duty. Entitlements to the following CRAs are reported into the Marine Corps Total Force System via unit diary entry for payment, per reference (g):

    a. Basic CRA (BCRA). BCRA is intended for enlisted Marines (both Regular and Reserve on extended active duty) in their first 3 years of active duty and computes to approximately 70 percent of Standard CRA (SCRA). BCRA accrues beginning with the first day of the month following the completion of 6 months continuous active duty without regard to time lost, from the date of last authorization to the Initial Issue. BCRA will continue to accrue during the remainder of the first 3 years of continuous active duty.

   b. Standard CRA (SCRA). SCRA is intended for enlisted Marines (both Regular and Reserve on extended active duty) serving beyond 3 years of active duty. SCRA will accrue to enlisted Marines beginning with the first day of the month following the completion of 36 months of active duty without regard to time lost, from the date of last authorization of the Initial Issue. This allowance will continue during the remainder of the period of continuous active duty.

3. Restriction on CRA accrual. Time served under one of the following circumstances does not count towards accrual of continuous active duty time (for either BCRA or SCRA) while:

   a. Serving in a temporary commissioned or warrant status.

   b. Pay is forfeited.

   c. CRA is suspended because a replacement in-kind process has been instituted during a declared combat period (extremely rare).

   d. Confined and sentenced to a punitive discharge at the expiration of the period of confinement.

   e. In a declared missing status.

   f. Serving active duty with another Service.

2007. CASH CLOTHING ALLOWANCES. Entitlements to the following clothing cash allowances are reported into the Marine Corps Total Force System for payment, per reference (g):

   • Civilian Clothing Monetary Allowances
   • Personal Items Allowance for Enlisted Women
   • Miscellaneous Enlisted Cash Clothing Allowances
   • Cash Allowances for Officers

1. Civilian Clothing Monetary Allowances. Civilian clothing
monetary allowances are provided to procure an initial allowance
of civilian clothing or replace civilian clothing for individuals
ordered by the CMC to wear civilian clothing more than half the
time performing official duties. Civilian clothing is defined as
clothing suitable for the duties being performed and may vary in
formality from business attire to casual clothing appropriate for
rugged field wear. All enlisted personnel meeting the
eligibility and conditions of entitlement may receive this
allowance. Only officers assigned to a permanent duty station
outside the United States are authorized to receive these
allowances. The allowances described in this section are
furnished in addition to other clothing allowances to which an
individual may be entitled, therefore CRA continues to accrue
while an enlisted Marine receives a civilian clothing monetary
allowance.

    a. Types of Civilian Clothing Monetary Allowances

        (1) Initial Permanent Duty Civilian Clothing Allowance.
This allowance is for Marines required to wear civilian clothes
more than half the time when performing official duty. This
allowance provides for civilian clothing required during the
first year of a permanent duty assignment.

        (2) Civilian Clothing Replacement Allowance. This is an
annual allowance intended to provide funds to individuals who
received the Initial Permanent Duty Civilian Clothing Allowance
and serve more than 1 year in positions requiring the wear of
civilian clothes. This allowance is payable at the end of the
anniversary month of the Marine commencing the qualifying
assignment if it is projected that he or she will serve at least
6 additional months in that assignment. The value of this
replacement allowance will not exceed one third of the Initial
Permanent Duty Civilian Clothing Allowance. The commanding
officer (CO) of Marine Security Guard Battalion (MSG Bn) may
elect to authorize an up-front payment of 2 years worth of this
replacement allowance along with the Initial Permanent Duty
Civilian Clothing Allowance, subject to the following
limitations:

        (a) This up-front payment is limited to one time in a
Marine's career.

(b) Marines who receive the up-front payment will not be authorized another Civilian Clothing Replacement Allowance until 3 years have elapsed from the date of the initial payment.

(3) <u>Temporary Additional Duty (TAD) Civilian Clothing Allowances</u>

(a) <u>Short Term TAD</u>. This allowance is authorized when civilian clothing is required in connection with TAD of at least 15 days (consecutive or cumulative) within a 30-day period. The value of this short term TAD allowance will not exceed one third of the Initial Permanent Duty Civilian Clothing Allowance.

(b) <u>Long Term TAD</u>. This allowance is authorized when civilian clothing is required in connection with TAD of at least 30 days (consecutive or cumulative) within a 36-month period. The value of this long term TAD allowance will not exceed two thirds of the Initial Permanent Duty Civilian Clothing Allowance.

b. <u>Eligibility</u>

(1) Enlisted personnel are eligible for civilian clothing monetary allowances while serving on extended active duty (more than 6 months of active duty) in one of the following capacities:

(a) White House duty, as determined by the military aide.

(b) Congressional escort duty, as determined by the CMC Office of Legislative Affairs (OLA).

(c) Intelligence, security, and related activities.

(d) Permanent or temporary duty in a foreign country when required by host government or U.S. ambassador (State Department duty).

(e) TAD or other service in an Explosive Ordnance Disposal (EOD) or an explosive detector dog handler unit, acting on behalf of the Secret Service.

(f) Law enforcement, military policy, or criminal investigative duty.

(g) As required by the CO.

(2) Regular officers and Reserve officers assigned to extended active duty (more than 6 months of active duty) are eligible for civilian clothing monetary allowances, if required, when permanently assigned to duty station outside of the United States (outside the 48 contiguous states, Alaska, Hawaii, and the District of Columbia).

c. Conditions of Entitlement. See figure 2-1 following.

d. Requests for Civilian Clothing Monetary Allowances

(1) COs must attest to the following conditions and provide in a written request to the PMCUB:

(a) Amount of time civilian clothing is required to be worn by the individual in the official capacity of his/her duty (approximate number of days or months)

(b) Individual's effective date of assignment to qualifying duty

(c) Individual's end of current contract date

(d) Individual's rotation date

(e) For officers, request must also include copy of Permanent Change of Station (PCS) orders

(2) Requests for each of the civilian clothing monetary allowances (except the Civilian Clothing Replacement Allowance – per paragraph 2007.1.d(6) following) must then be submitted to the PMCUB, via the Defense Finance and Accounting Service Center (DFAS), for written approval prior to running unit diary entries, per reference (g). Send requests to:

Commandant of the Marine Corps (CMC)
Permanent Marine Corps Uniform Board (PMCUB)
2200 Lester Street
Quantico, VA 22134-6050

via:

Defense Finance and Accounting Service (DFAS) Center
Support Services Division
Accounts Maintenance Section (PMCF)
Kansas City, MO 64197-0001

(3) Upon receipt, DFAS will review the individual's pay record to determine whether the individual previously received any civilian clothing allowances and endorse the request. The endorsement will indicate the amount and date of any such civilian clothing allowance which was authorized during the previous 3-year period, as specified by the conditions of entitlement provided in figure 2-1.

(4) Upon verification from DFAS, the PMCUB will determine whether a civilian clothing monetary allowance is authorized and will notify the command in writing. Only upon written approval from the PMCUB can the unit diary entry be made to initiate payment of the cash allowance per reference (g).

(5) The individual's CO will annually certify/recertify an individual's qualifications for the Civilian Clothing Replacement Allowance and upon approval report appropriate unit diary transaction per reference (g).

2. <u>Personal Items Allowance for Enlisted Women</u>. The Personal Items Allowance is a one-time cash allowance paid to supplement the Initial Issue to recruits/reenlistees. This allowance covers the purchase of underclothing, shoes, nylons, and other personal items not stocked within the supply system. This cash allowance is reported into the Marine Corps Total Force System for payment per reference (g).

3. <u>Miscellaneous Enlisted Cash Clothing Allowances</u>. Miscellaneous enlisted cash clothing allowances are cash allowances provided to unique organizations for the purchase of clothing items not stocked within the supply system. Typically, these allowances are paid to supplement gratuitous issues of clothing. Miscellaneous enlisted cash clothing allowances are listed annually in reference (c) and must be reported into the Marine Corps Total Force System for payment, per reference (g).

4. Cash Clothing Allowances for Officers. Officers are entitled
to two cash clothing allowances as reimbursement for the purchase
of required uniforms items (see reference (c)). These allowances
must be reported into the Marine Corps Total Force System for
payment per reference (g) and can be paid concurrently.

    a. Initial Uniform Allowance for Officers. This allowance
is payable only once to eligible officers, commissioned or
appointed in the Regular or Reserve components of the Marine
Corps. The Initial Uniform Allowance for officers is payable as
follows:

        (1) Upon first reporting for active duty (other than for
training) for a period of more than 90 days. A member entering
active duty as an officer in a Regular Component upon Reserve
Officer Training Corps (ROTC) graduation after October 12, 1964,
is considered to have entered on active duty for more than 90
days.

        (2) Upon completing at least 14 days of active duty or
active duty for training as a member of a Reserve Component.

        (3) Upon completing 14 periods of inactive-duty training
as a member of the Ready Reserve. Each period must be of at
least 2 hours duration.

        (4) Upon transfer from another service Reserve component.
Regular officers may not receive this allowance when transferring
from another military service.

        (5) If a member has received the Initial Uniform
Allowance in any amount as an officer under conditions other than
those listed in subparagraphs 2007.4a(1) through 2007.4a(4)
preceding, the member cannot again be entitled to this allowance.

        (6) Only periods of duty that require wearing of the
uniform are counted for entitlement to this allowance.

        (7) An officer must be determined physically qualified
for active duty before entitlement to this allowance accrues.

    b. Additional Active Duty Uniform Allowance for Officers.
The Additional Active Duty Uniform Allowance for officers is
payable to eligible officers commissioned in the Reserve

component and ROTC graduates appointed in the Regular component of the Marine Corps. The Additional Active Duty Uniform Allowance for officers is payable as follows:

(1) Each time of entry or reentry on active duty, or active duty for training (including authorized travel time) for more than 90 days. The period served may be under orders specifying active duty for more than 90 days or under two or more orders requiring a continuous period of more than 90 days' active duty.

(2) An officer commissioned in a Regular component upon ROTC graduation after October 12, 1964, accrues entitlement to the allowance on commencement of duty as a regular officer. The officer is considered then to have entered on active duty for more than 90 days.

(3) This allowance is not payable if the officer has received an initial uniform allowance of <u>more than</u> the current Additional Active Duty Uniform Allowance for officers during the current tour of active duty or within a period of 2 years before entering on that tour.

(4) This allowance is not payable when the tour of duty for which payment is being considered began within 2 years after the end of a previous period of active duty, or active duty for training, of more than 90 days. This applies whether or not a uniform allowance was paid for the previous tour of duty. It applies only if the prior service was performed as a Reserve officer or as a Regular officer commissioned upon ROTC graduation after October 12, 1964.

(5) A Reserve officer ordered to an indefinite tour of active duty or active duty for training is not entitled to this allowance until the member completes more than 90 days of that tour.

(6) Only periods of duty requiring the wearing of the uniform are counted for entitlement to the allowance prescribed in this paragraph.

(7) To be entitled under this paragraph, an officer must be determined physically qualified for active duty.

(8) For additional restrictions and examples on how to compute the 2-year period, see chapter 30 of reference (a).

2008. SUPPLEMENTARY CLOTHING ALLOWANCES. Supplementary clothing allowances are additional/extra clothing allowances authorized to enlisted personnel when they are assigned to a tour of duty that requires extra clothing for the performance of such duty. Supplementary clothing allowances are additional quantities or special items of uniform clothing not required by the majority of other enlisted personnel. Organizational clothing should also be considered as a means for providing additional, mission-specific uniform clothing, per chapter 7 of this Manual. Supplementary clothing allowances may not exceed 20 percent of the Initial Clothing Allowance established by the Assistant Secretary of Defense (ASD(FMP)).

1. Eligibility. Unit or activity commanders are responsible for verifying eligibility for a supplementary clothing allowance for enlisted personnel only as set forth in reference (c). Certification that the requesting individual's record has been checked and the individual is authorized to the allowance(s) is done by signing the Combined Individual Clothing Requisition and Issue Slip (NAVMC 604/604B) and subsequent documentation on the Individual Clothing Record (NAVMC 631/631A), per chapter 3 of this Manual. The unit/organization commander or his designee, authorized in writing to sign by-direction for the commander, must certify (sign) the NAVMC 604/604B. Only officers may be designated to sign NAVMC 604/604Bs, as these forms involve the direct expenditure of Government funds.

    a. Supplementary clothing allowances will be furnished to enlisted personnel prior to transfer to an organization which is authorized such allowances, per reference (c), with the following exceptions:

        (1) In those cases where a Marine Corps detachment is physically located at another service activity and/or the detachment is not authorized supply personnel within their table of organization to process clothing orders, the Officer in Charge (OIC) will issue a duplicate copy of the NAVMC 604/604B for insertion on top of the enlistment contract of the transferring individual's service record book (SRB) to ensure the gaining

command is aware of the requirement for subsequent issuance, citing this paragraph as authority for noncompliance with the provisions of chapter 3 following.

(2) Personnel assigned to MSG Bn, Quantico, VA, for duty with the Department of State will receive a supplementary clothing allowance only upon the satisfactory completion of a course of instruction and when actually assigned to the Department of State for duty.

(3) The Recruiters Blue Uniform Allowance will be issued to students immediately upon successful completion of the Recruiters School, MCRD, San Diego. When transfer orders are received and special measurement clothing is required, the clothing officer will forward the requisition and appropriate measurements to DSCP requesting that the special measurement clothing be forwarded to the CO of the organization to which the individual was transferred.

(4) Supplementary clothing allowances will not be issued prior to transfer of enlisted personnel to Marine Barracks, 8th and I Streets, S.E., Washington, DC, or to those Navy enlisted personnel who are authorized the special initial clothing allowances per paragraph 2004 preceding.

b.   Only one entitlement to the same type of allowance will accrue during any one period of continuous assignment to such duty. An individual who has received a supplementary clothing allowance will not be authorized a subsequent allowance of the same items upon assignment to duty requiring the wearing of uniform clothing for which the allowance is provided, if less than 3 years have elapsed between the effective date of the new assignment and the last day of the previous assignment to such duty.

c.   If the individual is transferred from a unit or duty which afforded an allowance to another unit or duty that provides for entitlement to a larger or different type of allowance than that initially furnished, the individual will be entitled to the difference between the two allowances, as appropriate. Additionally, if a supplementary clothing allowance increases for a unit or activity, all members assigned to that unit or activity that will be remaining more than 6 additional months will be issued the increase items (i.e., allowance will be "grand-fathered"), if so designated in the allowance approval document.

d. Grade insignia, service stripes, trouser stripes, and waistplates may be issued in conjunction with supplementary clothing allowances and sewn on (if applicable) using Operations and Maintenance, Marine Corps (O&MMC) funds, under the specific circumstances described in paragraph 2009.1 and figure 2-3 following.

e. Personnel who are furnished a supplementary clothing allowance will be permitted to retain such clothing upon transfer from the duty for which the clothing was authorized, provided they have served more than 6 months since the date of issue of the allowance.

2. Method of Issue. Most issues of supplementary clothing allowances will be made by authorized MCSSs or RCOs via the use of a NAVMC 604/604B. If a unit or activity is not supported by a MCSS or RCO, the supply officer must order and issue the authorized items, per figure 2-2 following. Specific instructions for accounting and record keeping for clothing allowance issues are provided in chapter 3 following.

3. Types of Supplementary Clothing Allowances. Supplementary clothing allowances consist of:

a. Maternity Uniform Allowance. The Maternity Uniform Allowance is authorized to pregnant enlisted Marines or enlisted Navy personnel serving with active Marine Corps units (who have elected to wear the Marine Corps uniform) who expect to remain on active duty or in an active Reserve status beyond the time when they can no longer wear the service/utility uniform properly.

(1) The Maternity Uniform Allowance is authorized only once during a 36-month period, commencing on the date of initial issuance.

(2) Enlisted Marines or Sailors are required to present to their CO a certificate of pregnancy, signed by a proper medical officer. This certificate of pregnancy must accompany the submission of form NAVMC 604B for the Maternity Uniform Allowance.

(3) Maternity Uniform Allowance issues shall be recorded on form NAVMC 631A, per chapter 3 of this Manual.

b. Blue Uniform Allowances. Blue uniform allowances are authorized to specified enlisted Marines required to wear the blue uniform as part of their assigned duties. Blue uniform allowances are issued in various compilations and quantities (small, medium, large, and recruiters issues), per reference (c). Marines who have been issued a supplementary blue uniform allowance will retain the issued items for 3 years after detachment from qualifying duty, regardless of whether or not the items are still serviceable. This will allow replacement of unserviceable items should an individual be assigned to subsequent duty which requires a supplementary blue uniform allowance issue.

c. Special Blue Uniform Replacement Allowance. The Special Blue Uniform Replacement Allowance is an authorization to replace unserviceable components of authorized supplementary blue uniform allowances, not a complete new issue of the applicable supplementary blue uniform allowance.

(1) Eligibility. This Special Blue Uniform Replacement Allowance is authorized to the following enlisted Marines under the conditions specified:

(a) Those assigned to career specialty duties only (recruiters in Military Occupational Specialty (MOS) 8412 and musicians in occupational field 55 and MOS 9812). This replacement of unserviceable blue uniform components is authorized every 3 years, beginning with the third anniversary of assignment to such duty.

(b) Those assigned to duty entitling them to a supplementary blue uniform allowance and less than 3 years have elapsed since their previous assignment wherein blues were required. This replacement of unserviceable blue uniform components is authorized at the beginning of each subsequent assignment to qualifying duty.

(c) Those assigned to duty entitling them to a supplementary blue uniform allowance and are subsequently extended on such duty beyond 3 years, including Marines on extended active duty (more than 6 months of active duty). This replacement of unserviceable blue uniform components is authorized on the third anniversary of assignment to such duty.

(d) Those transferred from a unit or duty which afforded a supplementary blue uniform allowance to another unit that provides for a supplementary blue uniform allowance. This replacement of unserviceable blue uniform components is authorized only for those items included in the new units allowance.

(2) Method of Issue

(a) Replacement on an item basis will be effected only if the individual has more than 6 months remaining on qualifying duty and will not exceed the types and quantities of items contained in the current applicable supplementary blue uniform allowance.

(b) Inspections of supplementary blue uniform allowance items will be conducted to determine serviceability. Personnel conducting inspections for Marines in career specialties 8412 and 9812 will be limited to COs of recruiting stations, band officers, and drum and bugle corps officers, as appropriate. Inspections for other authorized Marines will be conducted by the individual's CO. For those Marines who are geographically isolated from the command structure (e.g., Marine security guards), the senior Marine is authorized to conduct inspections for serviceability.

(c) All items designated as unserviceable for which replacement will be effected must be recovered by the supporting organic supply account and turned over to the local Defense Reutilization and Marketing Office (DRMO) for proper disposal.

(d) Recovery of the unserviceable item and issue of the replacement item will be recorded on the NAVMC 631/631A, per chapter 3 of this Manual.

d. Miscellaneous Uniform Allowances. Miscellaneous uniform allowances are authorized to enlisted Marines required to wear unique items or regular items more frequently than usual as part of their assigned duties. Miscellaneous uniform allowances are issued in various compilations and quantities as specified in reference (c) and must be maintained for a period of 3 years following authorized duty. Supplementary clothing allowance documentation and record keeping procedures apply.

4. Requests for Supplementary Clothing Allowances will be submitted to the PMCUB at the following address:

> Commandant of the Marine Corps (CMC)
> Permanent Marine Corps Uniform Board (PMCUB)
> 2200 Lester Street
> Quantico, VA 22134-6050

All requests must be signed by the CO and submitted via the chain of command for endorsement. Requests shall contain the following information: name and military address of the organization, reporting unit code, monitor command code, table of organization (T/O) number and date, line number(s) and billet description, tour length, recommended allowance (specify individual items required and/or type of allowance), number of Marines to be issued the allowance, and the justification. The following additional information, based on a 12-month period, is required, dependening on the type of clothing requested:

   a. Dress Blue Uniform Items. Number and description of various military ceremonies (indicating other commands involved), civil community functions, other public relations activities, and/or assigned duties when the blue uniform would be more appropriate than the service uniform, and the total number of hours involved during duty performance.

   b. All Other Uniforms/Items. Weather factors, duties involved, and available laundry/drycleaning facilities, services, and costs.

2009. OTHER CLOTHING ISSUES AND SERVICES. Clothing items and services gratuitously provided to authorized personnel, per the guidance in this section, are as follows:

   • Uniform Accessories
   • Uniform Alterations
   • Recruit Incentive Issues
   • Miscellaneous Issues to Absentees, Deserters, Prisoners, or Personnel Discharged Under Exceptional Circumstances

- Issues to Hospitalized Personnel
- Issues for the Burial of the Dead
- Replacement Issues Under the Personal Property Claims
  Regulations
- Other Replacement Issues

1. Uniform Accessories. Uniform accessories, including grade insignia, service stripes, trousers stripes, and waistplates, will be gratuitously issued per the following guidance:

    a. Figure 2-3 following lists authorized accessories and occasions authorized for issuance. The quantities to be issued will be based on the amount of items in the current applicable MRL and any other additional allowance required to be possessed and maintained by the individual. When a supplementary clothing allowance is issued, the quantities of grade insignia and/or stripes to be issued will be limited to the quantities required to compliment those items contained in the supplementary clothing allowance.

    b. Funding Source. Authorized uniform accessories will be financed by unit or HQMC O&MMC appropriations, except those specifically identified as being funded by MILPERS appropriations, per figure 2-3 following. The expense of additional grade insignia, service stripes, trousers stripes, or waistplates in excess of authorized quantities or to replace those worn out will be borne by the individual. Sewing on at Government expense is not authorized for other occasions to include gratuitous issues of accessories, additional promotions, time-in-service being met, etc. Under these circumstances, the sewing on will be at the expense of the individual.

    c. Method of Issue. Issues are to be made using forms NAVMC 604/604B, per figure 2-2 following, using the proper appropriation data from the funding source identified in figure 2-3 following. Units may also purchase uniform accessories in bulk from the local MCSS, supply permitting, for issue via forms NAVMC 604/604B to authorized individuals. Gratuitous issues must be further documented on forms NAVMC 631/631A, per chapter 3 of this Manual.

2. Uniform Alterations. Uniform alterations are authorized to obtain an improved fit and still retain a smart military

appearance, per reference (i), but will not change the intended appearance or function of the garment. However, stocks of altered clothing are not desirable and should be avoided to the maximum extent possible. Local tailors should be cautioned not to cut away excess material when performing alterations, in order that future necessary realterations may be accomplished. Uniform fit alterations and other alteration services required to sew on authorized uniform accessories will be provided per the following guidance:

    a. Gratuitous Alterations. Articles of outer uniform clothing provided the individual (except commissioned officers and warrant officers) from Government supply sources, including recovered clothing, shall be gratuitously altered to fit the individual at the time of sale or issue. However, such alterations shall not be made if the cost exceeds 50 percent of the standard price of the item being issued or sold. Alteration costs which exceed 50 percent of a recovered clothing item being sold will be borne by the individual. This cost limitation does not apply to initial issues made at the the MCRDs or the Marine Corps Combat Development Command (MCCDC) during initial training. Additional gratuitous alteration services and the occasions they are authorized are listed in figure 2-3 following.

    b. Profile Changes

        (1) Profile changes following initial training may make alterations necessary for initially issued items of outer uniform clothing. These alterations may be performed at Government expense up to 6 months after the individual reports to his/her first permanent duty assignment, per figure 2-3 following. Outer clothing includes service and dress trousers, service and dress shirts, dress coats, and utility coats and trousers; it does not include sweaters or footwear.

        (2) When physical profile changes up to 6 months after reporting to the first permanent duty assignment are such that garments cannot be altered to obtain an acceptable fit or the alteration costs would exceed the cost of a new garment, replacement of such garments is authorized. Issues shall be made from stocks of serviceable recovered clothing, whenever possible. The exchanged clothing will be recovered by the issuing organization.

(3) Alteration costs shall not exceed 50 percent of the price of the item being reissued. Such replacement issue shall be made upon certification by the officer in charge (OIC) of the MCSS/RCO that replacement issue is more economical than alterations and shall be approved by the individual's commander. Utility uniforms cannot be altered, so a replacement (with recovery of non-fitting utilities) is authorized. The serviceability of the recovered clothing should be inspected and gross negligence should be reported to the individual's command for investigation.

(4) For profile changes related to a medical condition, see paragraph 6005.1.c following.

c. Funding. Authorized gratuitous uniform alterations will be provided using O&MMC appropriations, per figure 2-3 following.

(1) Alterations to uniform clothing issued or sold over the counter or by mail order by an MCSS/RCO, will be performed under a contract/agreement between the store and the alteration service provider. Request for alterations of mail order uniform clothing must be accompanied by a copy of the mail order receipt. Some organizations that do not have access to a MCSS/RCO have local contract alteration services available.

(2) If unusual circumstances prevent initial alterations at the time and place of issue or sale, a memorandum, signed by the OIC of the MCSS/RCO, identifying the garment and explaining why alterations were not accomplished shall be provided to the individual. This memorandum will authorize the alterations at Government expense at the individual's next duty station. In the case of organizations that do not have access to a MCSS/RCO, the memorandum must include appropriation data to fund the alterations. If no funding appropriation is provided, gratuitous alterations will not be performed.

d. Alteration Sources. Every effort shall be made to provide all personnel proper tailoring facilities. Alterations for Reserve personnel are detailed in paragraph 8006 of this Manual. Personnel shall be advised that alterations performed at other than designated military tailoring establishments shall be the individual's responsibility and subject to strict conformance to published Marine Corps regulations. Alterations made to outer uniform clothing of individuals on duty at a location where contract alteration services are not available shall be paid for by the individuals concerned. The following statement, if applicable, shall be completed by the individual and forwarded to the parent organization for reimbursement:

"I (name, grade, and SSN) HEREBY CERTIFY that I paid the attached bill for alterations to outer uniform clothing and that such alterations were in accordance with current Marine Corps regulations.

"It is, therefore, requested that the undersigned be reimbursed in the amount of $_____, United States currency.

_____
"(Signature)"

NOTE: If foreign currency was used to pay for the alterations, an official of the United States must certify the rate of exchange (on date of payment) of United States currency against foreign currency as follows:

"I (name, position, and title) HEREBY CERTIFY that the amount of the attached bill (amount in foreign currency) does convert to $_____, United States currency."

e. Marine Security Guard Battalion (MSGBn) Alterations. The CO, MSGBn, Quantico, VA, is authorized to approve payment of clothing alterations for system uniform clothing issued to/purchased by enlisted Marines serving in overseas duty assignments not serviced by a contractable alterations facility. Funding will be provided from the current MSGBn's O&MMC appropriations. In any instance where the cost of alterations exceeds the maximum allowable ceiling (50 percent of the unit price of the article), the embassy or detachment commander shall provide certification to the fact that the expenses are fair and reasonable for the location. Additionally, a copy of each approved authorization shall be provided to the CMC (LPC).

f. Repair, Laundering, and Drycleaning. The repair, laundering, and/or drycleaning of all gratuitously issued clothing items are the responsibilities of the individual. Under no circumstances will these services be provided at Government expense. This policy does not pertain to organizational issues discussed in chapter 7 following.

3. Recruit Incentive Issues. There are two uniform incentive issues offered at recruit training, dress blue uniform issues to recruit honor graduates and Delayed Entry Program recruits who make three qualifying referrals. Both issues are for one complete dress blue uniform, minus any dress blue uniform items issued as part of the Initial Issue (seabag). If the following issues cannot be made prior to an eligible recruit leaving the MCRD, issued items must be shipped to the recruit's next duty station. Gratuitous issue at the next duty station is not authorized, unless funding is provided in advance. Entitlement to either of these issues will not affect entitlement to subsequent issues of dress blue uniforms for allowance issues.

    a. Recruit Honor Graduate. Per reference (j), MCRDs may use local O&MMC appropriations to present a dress blue uniform to recruit honor graduates. Proper entries must be made in the individual's official military personnel file (OMPF).

    b. Delayed Entry Program (DEP). Per reference (k), the Marine Corps Recruiting Command (MCRC) authorizes and funds an incentive issue of the blue dress uniform to members of the DEP who refer three individuals. Recruiting Station CO's must certify authorized individuals using form DD 1966 and forward authorization to the MCRD. The individual making the referrals will be eligible for this dress blue uniform issue only if those referrals enlist in to the DEP or directly into the Marine Corps or SMCR (including awaiting Initial Active Duty Training), prior to the individual's graduation from recruit training. Entitlement to presentation of a dress blue uniform as an honor graduate nullifies entitlement to this DEP referral incentive issue.

4. Miscellaneous Issues to Absentees, Deserters, Prisoners or Personnel Discharged Under Exceptional Circumstances

    a. Issues to Marine Corps Absentees and Deserters

        (1) Returning absentees and deserters who return to their parent command and are awaiting adjudication that have not been transferred to the brig will be required to purchase only a minimum amount of uniform clothing items necessary to maintain acceptable standards of personal appearance; they will not be issued or required to purchase an entire new MRL of clothing.

Serviceable uniform clothing should first be purchased from available stocks of recovered clothing, then from limited or substitute standard item stock or from oldest standard stock.

(2) Returning absentees and deserters who voluntarily report to a nonparent command will be required to purchase a minimum amount of uniform clothing items necessary to maintain acceptable standards of personal appearance until they have been transferred to their parent command and restored to a full duty status. Serviceable uniform clothing should first be purchased from available stocks of recovered clothing, then from limited or substitute standard item stock or from oldest standard stock. When it has been determined by the commander that a returning absentee or deserter attached to another command does not have access to sufficient funds for the purchase of required clothing, a checkage sale shall be processed to provide required clothing. The commander who approves the checkage shall ensure that the completed form NAVMC 604/604B is forwarded, by cover letter, to the commander of the individual's parent command in order that the checkage may be processed against the applicable pay record.

(3) Individuals restored to a full duty status, after clothing has been recovered per chapter 6 of this Manual, shall be issued those items indicated on the certificate of inventory contained in the individual's OMPF as having been recovered in a serviceable condition. If the required inventory is missing, required items will be funded by the unit whose responsibility it was to conduct the inventory; O&MMC funded vice MILPERS funded. Worn gloves, underclothing, and socks which have been recovered will not be gratuitously replaced for the individual. The quantities of clothing which will be provided the individual under this authority will not exceed the amounts contained in the current MRL.

(a) Recovered clothing should be used for these issues. If recovered clothing is not available, issues may be made first from limited or substitute standard item stock, then from oldest standard stock.

(b) The individual will be required to purchase those items still required after the preceding issue has been made, in order to bring the quantity of clothing in that person's possession up to the current MRL.

b. Issues to Marine Corps Prisoners

    (1) When courts-martial prisoners are transferred and they do not possess the necessary traveling uniform, a suitable portion of the Minimum Traveling Uniform, per paragraph 9004.2 of this Manual, less insignia, will be issued and accounted for as a "miscellaneous issue/replacement issue," per figure 3-1 and paragraph 6005.1 of this Manual.

        (a) The traveling uniform will be expended from the individual's clothing account. The expenditure document will include the individual's name, SSN, and a statement to the effect that the clothing has been issued to provide a necessary traveling uniform to a courts-martial prisoner.

        (b) Recovered clothing should be used for these issues. If recovered clothing is not available, issues may be made first from limited or substitute standard item stock, then from oldest standard stock.

    (2) Personnel confined to brigs on shore which are under Marine Corps jurisdiction will be required to have in their possession certain articles of individual uniform clothing as prescribed for prisoners in the particular confinement facility, per reference (1). When clothing other than that listed in the current MRL is required, the brig will notify the committing command. Personnel who are in a pay status but who do not have the required items of clothing will be provided necessary articles on a cash and/or checkage sales basis. For personnel in a non-pay status that have not been properly equipped by their parent command, the brig will provide for this issue, per reference (1), using local O&MMC funds and may seek reimbursement from the parent command.

    (3) Prisoners granted emergency leave may be issued a portion of the Minimum Traveling Uniform, per paragraph 9004.2 of this Manual, necessary for travel and charged accordingly. If the individual granted emergency leave is in a non-pay status, the issue rendered the individual will be expended from the account as a "miscellaneous issue/replacement issue," per figure 3-1 and paragraph 6005.1 of this Manual. Upon return from such leave, the clothing furnished the individual will be applied against the clothing allowance to which the individual may be entitled, or, if the individual is not entitled to a clothing allowance, the outer garments furnished will be recovered.

(4) <u>Prisoners awaiting authority to be restored to duty</u>
<u>or awaiting action by the Judge Advocate General of the Navy or</u>
<u>appellate review</u> may be issued a portion of the Minimum Traveling
Uniform, per paragraph 9004.2 of this Manual, necessary to
maintain acceptable standards of personal appearance. If the
prisoner is in a non-pay status, the issue rendered the
individual will be expended from the account as a "miscellaneous
issue/replacement issue" per figure 3-1 and paragraph 6005.1
following. If authority is subsequently received to restore the
individual to a full duty status, the clothing issued under the
foregoing authority will be deducted from the remainder of the
clothing to which the individual may be entitled. If the
individual is not restored to a full duty status and is not
otherwise entitled to an issue of clothing, then all outer
garments furnished will be recovered.

    c. <u>Issues to Prisoners/Detainees from Services other than</u>
<u>Marine Corps</u>. A Minimum Traveling Uniform, per paragraph 9004.2
of this Manual, may be issued when the activity commander
determines that the health and comfort or appearance of the
individual warrants such an issue. Local O&MMC funds will be
used for this issue and reported as an "Issue for Other
Purposes." Normally, however, individuals who surrender or are
apprehended will be returned to their parent service in the
clothing worn at the time of return to military jurisdiction.

    d. <u>Issues to Personnel Discharged Under Exceptional</u>
<u>Circumstances</u>. Individuals discharged for the reasons set forth
in paragraph 6003 following may be issued non-distinct items from
the Minimum Traveling Uniform, per paragraph 9004.2 of this
Manual, or appropriate civilian clothing for wear to their home.

    (1) Nondistinct uniform clothing items are the belt,
buckle, shirt (without insignia), skirt, slacks, trousers, etc.
The all-weather coat with insignia of grade removed may be issued
at the direction of the CO when weather conditions require. The
quantity and unit of issue for any item is one each. The issue
rendered will be expended from the account as a "miscellaneous
issue/replacement issue," per figure 3-1 and paragraph 6005.1 of
this Manual.

    (2) Civilian clothing is limited to trousers/slacks,
sport shirt, blouse, and the like, only if required to suitably
clothe the

2009   INDIVIDUAL CLOTHING REGULATIONS

individual with respect to the season. The quantity and unit of issue for any item is one each. The cost will be charged to unit O&MMC appropriations, per reference (m). The decision to issue civilian clothing vice uniform clothing must be made in writing by the CO. The order will list the articles to be procured and issued and will reference this paragraph as authorization. Copies of receipts will be vouchered to the property records for record purposes only. They will have attached thereto a receipt signed by the dischargee and a copy of the CO's order. The original receipt will be attached to the CO's order as the authority for such purchase.

5. Issues to Hospitalized Personnel. Issues to hospitalized personnel are authorized for enlisted Marines who are not in possession of their uniform clothing due to medical evacuation and/or hospitalization. The issue shall consist of the minimum amount of uniform clothing necessary to maintain acceptable standards of personal appearance, up to the Minimum Traveling Uniform, per paragraph 9004.2 of this Manual. This issue will be expended as a "miscellaneous issue/replacement issue," per figure 3-1 and paragraph 6005.1 of this Manual (using MILPERS appropriations).

6. Issues for the Burial of the Dead. Issues for the burial of the dead are authorized to Marines on active duty or other eligible decedent (excluding retired or discharged personnel), per the reference (n), if the decedent's uniforms are not available or suitable for burial purposes. The preferred burial uniform for deceased Marines is the blue uniform (white gloves may be obtained for damaged hands). If the blue uniform is not available, the service uniform will be used. Issue should be made with new uniforms if at all possible.

    a. Officers. Items of system uniform clothing, such as socks, shoes, and underclothing, shall be issued and accounted for via a "miscellaneous issue/replacement issue," per figure 3-1 and paragraph 6005.1 of this Manual. Uniform items and accessories peculiar to officers, including the cover, appropriate grade insignia, and ribbon bars, will be provided by the local MCX, NEXCOM, AAFES or other authorized clothing sales store upon request by the CO. The next of kin of a retired or discharged individual authorized to wear Marine Corps uniforms may purchase the necessary uniform for the decedent for burial purposes only upon presentation of DD Form 256/DD Form 214 to the authorized clothing sales store. At commands where no MCX is available, the unit supply officer should contact Navy Mortuary Affairs at 1-888-647-6676 to discuss funding and/or possible reimbursement for the preferred burial uniform, per reference (o).

b. Enlisted Personnel. Necessary uniforms, including underclothing, socks, cap, shoes, appropriate grade insignia, and service stripes, will be provided and accounted for via a "miscellaneous issue/replacement issue," per figure 3-1 and paragraph 6005.1 of this Manual. Ribbons, ribbon bars, and badges will be provided by the MCX, NEXCOM, AAFES or other authorized clothing sales store. The next of kin of a retired or discharged individual authorized to wear Marine Corps uniforms may purchase the necessary uniform for the decedent for burial purposes only upon presentation of DD Form 256/DD Form 214 to the authorized clothing sales store. At commands where no MCX is available, the unit supply officer should contact Navy Mortuary Affairs at 1-888-647-6676 to discuss funding and/or possible reimbursement for the preferred burial uniform, per NAVMEDCOM 5360.1 (Decedent Affairs Manual).

c. Burial in Civilian Clothing. Upon request from the next of kin, a deceased Marine may be buried in personal civilian clothing or clothing provided by the next of kin. Civilian clothing may not be provided or reimbursed at Government expense, if the next of kin refuses to use available or offered uniforms. Reimbursement for civilian clothing is allowable if a uniform is not obtainable without undue delay.

7. Replacement Issues Under the Personal Property Claims Regulations. Replacement issues under the Personal Property Claims Regulations are those replacements which are made to personnel for damage, loss, destruction, capture, or abandonment of uniform clothing incident to military service, beyond normal wear and tear. Reference (p) dictates the policy for handling personal property claims, as follows:

a. Authorized Personal Property Claims. Claims submitted under this instruction will include only articles of individual uniform clothing. Should an individual desire to submit a claim for other personal property, a separate claim covering non-system clothing items must be submitted. Authorized personal property claims for uniform clothing are provided in figure 2-4 following. Officers may submit a personal property claim for damaged, lost, destroyed, captured, or abandoned uniform clothing, but replacement issues are only authorized for system clothing, not officer unique commercial clothing items.

   b. Personal Property Claims Not Considered.

      (1) Depreciation. Since replacement is made on an item basis, a depreciation factor is not to be used. The issuing officer merely enters the current standard cost of a replaced item under the "endorsements of issue" portion of the claim forms.

      (2) Losses by Postal Authorities. Claims based on the loss of property after it has been delivered to the post office for shipment to the owner do not come within the purview of this policy. Such claims are a matter for adjudication by postal authorities under the provisions of the post office manual, or by the Judge Advocate General of the Navy under the Navy General Claims Regulations.

      (3) Damage to or destruction of uniform clothing by battery acid, barbed wire, or sprayed paint, etc. while engaged in duties for which utility clothing is normally intended does not meet the conditions set forth in this or any other class of claim.

      (4) Loss or Damage When Under Owner's Control. The Government's obligation does not extend to property in the custody or under the control of the owner. The owner of the property has an obligation to safeguard said property and any loss or damage caused, in whole or in part, by active or passive negligence of the owner is not payable.

      (5) Property Stolen From Lockers. Replacement on an item basis of clothing stolen from a locker or other storage space used by the claimant will not be approved by the adjudicating authorities if based on the stated belief of investigating officers the Government was negligent in not providing storage with adequate locks.

      (6) Losses in Base/Station Laundries. Claims based on loss of clothing in Marine Corps base/station laundries are not payable.

(7) <u>Losses by Absentees and Deserters</u>. Replacement of clothing, based on separation of the owners from their property because of unauthorized absence, is prohibited.

c. <u>Actions Required Prior to Submission of a Personal Property Claim</u>

(1) <u>Investigation of Losses</u>. In instances of claims for replacement of clothing that is missing, action is to be taken to show that a loss has occurred. Acceptance of the claimant's statement of the loss should be contingent upon the results of the investigation or search instituted by the investigating officer.

(2) <u>Claim Processed with Carrier</u>. In those cases where a commercial carrier appears to bear liability for the loss and/or damage, a claim must first be filed against that carrier, prior to submission of a personal property claim. Checks received in settlement of claims arising under these provisions will be forwarded to DC, M&RA (MRP), together with a copy of the personal property claim and form NAVMC 604/604B effecting replacement.

(3) <u>Claim Processed with Personal Insurer</u>. The instructions contained in the preceding paragraph regarding losses recoverable from carriers are equally applicable when the property is insured. A claim for personal insurance should be processed and a copy of settlement provided before submitting a personal property claim.

(4) <u>Completion of Claim Forms With or Without Exhibits</u>. Ensure that all portions of the personal property claims form DD 1842 are complete, to include a full and complete statement of the circumstances which led to the submission of the claim.

d. <u>How to Submit a Personal Property Claim</u>. Personal Property Claims, utilizing form DD 1842, must be submitted to the DC, M&RA (MRP). Individuals may also submit personal property claims via the DC, M&RA website at www.manpower.usmc.mil, by selecting the "Personal and Family Readiness (MR)" link, then the "Personal Property Claims" link. This site also has a very thorough set of instructions for submitting personal property claims. A copy of the NAVMC 604/604B identifying the system uniform clothing items being claimed must be provided with the personal property claims forms. DC, M&RA (MRP) will assign an adjudicating authority for consideration of the claim.

e. Processing of Personal Claims for Replacement Issue

(1) Following adjudication, if the claim is authorized, proper documentation for processing with the NAVMC 604/604B will be provided by DC, M&RA (MRP). System uniform clothing items listed on the current MRL will be denied for personal property claim cash reimbursement and thus will be authorized for gratuitous replacement issue via form NAVMC 604/604B (using FAN 72048), per figure 3-1 of this Manual. The issue of items other than those authorized by the claim is not authorized.

(2) Once replacement issue has been effected on the approved claim, an authorized clothing officer will endorse the claim indicating the action accomplished, as well as ensure completion of the NAVMC 604/604B. The clothing so issued will be expended from the account and documented as a "Personal Property Claims Issue," per figure 3-1 of this Manual. A copy of the personal property claim should be filed with the NAVMC 604/604B.

f. Distribution of Personal Property Claims Forms

(1) Every effort will be made to settle all claims by initially effecting a complete issue as indicated by the approved claim. In those cases when the claim can be settled with the first issue, the original of the personal property claim will be retained by the clothing officer to support the clothing officer's retained copy of the NAVMC 604/604 documenting the clothing issued. One completed copy of all documents will be furnished the activity commander, for proper documentation per chapter 3 of this Manual. Copies of all completed documents shall also be forwarded to DC, M&RA (MRP).

(2) In those cases when only a partial issue can be effected at the first attempted settlement of the claim, the clothing officer making the partial issue will cause three additional certified copies of the claim to be prepared. The clothing officer will indicate such partial issue by endorsing the personal property claim accordingly. The quantity issued will be documented on the NAVMC 604/604B. Distribution of applicable documents will be as follows:

(a) Two certified copies of the NAVMC 604/604B and personal property claim forms will be forwarded to the activity commander; one copy to be provided to service member and a copy for the official files of the organization. The activity commander will prepare a new NAVMC 604/604B for issue to the individual for the items that were not available for issue.

        (b) One certified copy of the completed NAVMC 604/604B and personal property claim form will be submitted to DC, M&RA (MRP).

        (c) The original completed NAVMC 604/604B will be retained by the clothing officer to support the retained copy of the reported transaction.

        (3) In those unusual circumstances when a claim is not settled by two partial issues, the clothing officer making the second partial issue will prepare three additional certified copies of all the documents and make distribution of the claim forms as prescribed for partial issues.

8. <u>Other Replacement Issues</u>. See paragraph 6005 following.

INDIVIDUAL CLOTHING REGULATIONS

Type of Allowance	Conditions of Entitlement
Initial Permanent Duty Civilian Clothing Allowance	1. Must be individual's permanent duty station. 2. Individual must be required to wear civilian clothing more than 50% of the time. 3. Must be individual's first year of assignment. 4. Effective date is the date of assignment to authorized duty. 5. Allowance will not be paid again unless there is a 1 year break in authorized duty. Instead, individuals may be authorized a Civilian Clothing Replacement Allowance. 6. Individual must have more than 6 months of obligated service remaining and it is anticipated that individual will continue to serve in a qualifying duty for more than 6 months. Reservists are not entitled to this allowance unless they serve on extended active duty (more than 6 months continuous active duty). 7. If individual received a TAD Civilian Clothing Allowance within the preceding 12 months of commencing a qualifying permanent duty assignment, individual will be entitled to the difference between the TAD allowance amount received and the Initial Permanent Duty Civilian Clothing Allowance. 8. Officers are not entitled to this allowance unless assigned to a permanent duty station located outside the U.S.
Civilian Clothing Replacement Allowance	1. Individual must have received the Initial Permanent Duty Civilian Clothing Allowance and serve more than 1 year in authorized duty. 2. If reassigned to a qualifying duty, time since last payment of an Initial Permanent Duty Civilian Clothing Allowance must be less than 3 years. 3. If individual has a break between qualifying assignments, break must be less than 12 months. 4. If 2 or 3 above pertain, effective date is date reassigned or the anniversary of the date of any previous civilian clothing allowance, whichever occurs later. 5. Individual must have more than 6 months of obligated service remaining and it is anticipated that individual will continue to serve in qualifying duty for more than 6 months.

Figure 2-1.--Civilian Clothing Monetary Allowances
Conditions of Entitlement.

Type of Allowance	Conditions of Entitlement
Temporary Additional Duty (TAD) Civilian Clothing Allowances	1. Individual must be required to wear civilian clothing more than 50% of the time while TAD for 15 days in a 30-day period or 30 days in a 36-month period (consecutive or cumulative). 2. The 15-day qualification does not apply to EOD and EOD canine handling personnel, Defense Courier Service couriers, and On-Site Inspection Agency military personnel, who receive the Long Term TAD Civilian Clothing Allowance for 30 days upon their initial TAD travel requirement. 3. Maximum amount payable for all TAD performed in any 36-month period will not exceed the maximum prescribed for the 30-day period. The 30-day allowance payment will be less any amount paid within the past 36-month period for TAD. 4. Not authorized to Marines who received an Initial Permanent Duty Civilian Clothing Allowance or a Civilian Clothing Replacement Allowance within 12 months of performing a qualifying period of TAD. 5. Reservists are not entitled to this allowance unless they serve more than 6 months continuous active duty. 6. Officers are not entitled to this allowance unless assigned to a permanent duty station located outside the U.S.

Figure 2-1.--Civilian Clothing Monetary Allowances
Conditions of Entitlement—continued.

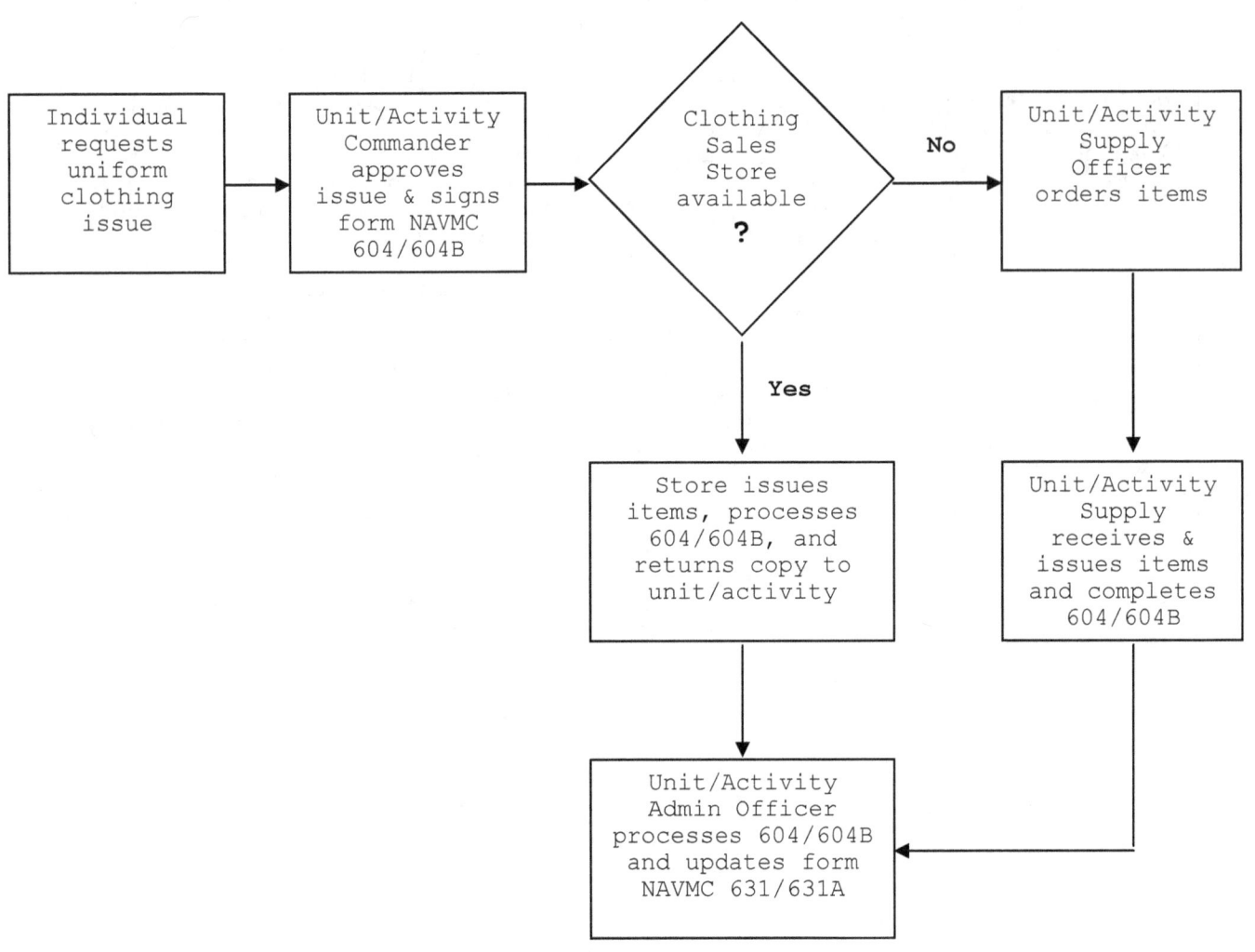

Figure 2-2.--Uniform Clothing Issue Process.

Item	Activity	Occasion	Funding Source
Alteration **(If cost is less than 50% U/P)**	Altered for Fit	1. Initial clothing allowance. 2. Supplementary allowance. 3. Personal property claims replacement. 4. Up to 6 months after reporting to the first permanent duty assignment following initial training when: a. Individual's profile changes. b. Replacement issue is made upon discovery of defective uniform clothing items. 5. New purchase. 6. Recovered clothing purchase. 7. Other clothing issues, per paragraph 2009 preceding. 8. Organizational/CTEP issue. 9. Specific return from combat.	O&MMC O&MMC O&MMC O&MMC O&MMC O&MMC O&MMC O&MMC O&MMC
Grade Insignia	Issued	1. Initial clothing allowance. 2. Supplementary allowance. 3. Personal property claims replacement. 4. <u>First</u> promotion to grade; additionally, (5) pairs of plastic Marine Corps grade insignia will be issued gratuitously upon promotion and (1) pair of plastic Navy grade insignia for each combat utility coat issued to authorized Navy personnel serving with Marine units and upon promotion. 5. Other clothing issues, per paragraph 2009 preceding. 6. Meritorious promotions during recruit training (service coats and shirts). 7. Organizational/CTEP issue. 8. Specific return from combat.	O&MMC O&MMC MILPERS O&MMC MILPERS O&MMC O&MMC MILPERS

Figure 2-3.--Uniform Accessories and Alterations.

INDIVIDUAL CLOTHING REGULATIONS

Item	Activity	Occasion	Funding Source
Grade Insignia	Sewn On	1. Initial clothing allowance.	O&MMC
		2. <u>First</u> supplementary allowance issue.	O&MMC
		3. Personal property claims replacement.	O&MMC
		4. Up to 6 months after reporting to the first permanent duty assignment following initial training when: a. Individual's profile changes. b. Replacement issue is made upon discovery of defective uniform clothing items.	O&MMC
		5. Other clothing issues, per paragraph 2009 preceding.	O&MMC
		6. Meritorious promotions during recruit training (service coats and shirts).	O&MMC
		7. Organizational/CTEP issue.	O&MMC
		8. Specific return from combat.	O&MMC
Martial Arts Belt	Issued	1. As qualified or replaced.	O&MMC
		2. Personal property claims replacement	MILPERS
		3. Other clothing issues, per paragraph 2009 preceding.	MILPERS
		4. Organizational/CTEP issue.	O&MMC
		5. Specific return from combat.	MILPERS
Name/Service Tapes	Issued	1. Initial clothing allowance.	MILPERS
		2. Supplementary allowance.	MILPERS
		3. Personal property claims replacement.	MILPERS
		4. Other clothing issues, per paragraph 2009 preceding.	MILPERS
		5. Organizational/CTEP issue.	O&MMC
		6. Specific return from combat.	MILPERS
Name/Service Tapes	Sewn On	1. Initial clothing allowance.	O&MMC
		2. Supplementary allowance.	O&MMC
		3. Personal property claims replacement.	O&MMC
		4. Other clothing issues, per paragraph 2009 preceding.	O&MMC
		5. Organizational/CTEP issue.	O&MMC
		6. Specific return from combat.	O&MMC
Service Stripes Trouser Stripes	Issued	1. Initial clothing allowance.	O&MMC
		2. Supplementary allowance.	O&MMC
		3. Upon reaching time-in-service (service stripes).	O&MMC
		4. <u>First</u> promotion to NCO (trouser stripes).	O&MMC
		5. Personal property claims replacement.	MILPERS
		6. Other clothing issues, per paragraph 2009 preceding.	MILPERS
		7. Organizational/CTEP issue.	O&MMC
		8. Specific return from combat.	MILPERS

Figure 2-3.--Uniform Accessories and Alterations—continued.

Item	Activity	Occasion	Funding Source
Service Stripes Trouser Stripes	Sewn On	1. Initial clothing allowance.	O&MMC
		2. First supplementary allowance.	O&MMC
		3. Personal property claims replacement.	O&MMC
		4. Other clothing issues, per paragraph 2009 preceding.	O&MMC
		5. Organizational/CTEP issue.	O&MMC
		6. Specific return from combat.	O&MMC
Waistplate w/ Insignia	Issued	1. Initial clothing allowance.	MILPERS
		2. Supplementary allowance.	MILPERS
		3. First promotion to grade while in billet requiring the wear of blue uniform.	O&MMC
		4. Personal property claims replacement.	MILPERS
		5. Other clothing issues, per paragraph 2009 preceding.	MILPERS
		6. Organizational/CTEP issue.	O&MMC
		7. Specific return from combat.	MILPERS

Figure 2-3.--Uniform Accessories and Alterations—continued.

INDIVIDUAL CLOTHING REGULATIONS

Claim Type	Major Elements Considered or Required
Claims in General	1. Proximate cause of the loss, damage, destruction, or abandonment was the negligent act or omission of agents or employees of the Government acting within the scope of their employment. 2. Loss, damage, destruction, or abandonment occurred incident to the service of the claimant.
Losses at Assigned Government Quarters or Other Authorized Places	1. Damage or destruction caused by fire, flood, hurricane, or an occurrence of equally serious importance. 2. Location must be designated by superior authority for the reception of the damage or destroyed property. 3. Loss of property through pilferage, theft, or damage when the property is located at a place designated by superior authority for the reception of such property, such as a warehouse, hospital, or baggage dump, or losses or damage arising from the separation of the owner from this property by reason of emergency hospitalization or similar emergencies where the Government is obligated to secure and safeguard the property. 4. Presupposes that there existed an obligation on the part of the Government, or its agents or employees to safeguard the property of the claimant.
Theft from Possession of Claimant	1. Positive evidence must exist to establish that the claimant exercised due care in the protection of such claimant's clothing and that a larceny, burglary, or housebreaking has occurred. 2. Location must be in assigned Government quarters or other authorized place designated by superior authority for the reception of the stolen property.
Transportation and Storage Losses	1. Travel, storage, or shipment involved was either under orders, in connection with orders, or in the performance of military duty. 2. No element of negligence on the part of the claimant exists when the loss arises while the property is in the claimant's personal custody and/or incident to transportation by a private conveyance. 3. Loss, damage, or destruction arises incident to the act of transportation, storage, or shipment of the property. 4. Losses while traveling under orders authorizing a delay en route, when items are in the custody of a Marine owner (or carrier) at the time of loss, damage, or destruction.

Figure 2-4.--Authorized Personal Property Claims.

2-44

Claim Type	Major Elements Considered or Required
Unusual Occurrence	1. Damage or loss must be a direct result of extraordinary risk, differentiated from normal risk. 2. Property is subjected to this risk by the performance of official noncombatant duties by the claimant. 3. Official noncombatant duties included efforts to save Government property or human life, or performance of duty in connection with civil disturbances, public disorders, and public disasters. 4. Property has been abandoned or destroyed as opposed to discarded, when such abandonment or destruction was ordered by superior authority or necessitated by military emergency "Abandonment" is not to be interpreted to cover the act of discarding property.
Property Used for the Benefit of the Government	Property (so used or held for use for the benefit of the Government at the direction or request of superior authority or by reason of military necessity) is not property being used for the purpose for which it was intended.

Figure 2-4.--Authorized Personal Property Claims—continued.

INDIVIDUAL CLOTHING REGULATIONS

CHAPTER 3

ACCOUNTING AND RECORD KEEPING

INDIVIDUAL CLOTHING REGULATIONS

CHAPTER 3

ACCOUNTING AND RECORD KEEPING

3000. <u>INTRODUCTION</u>. This chapter contains policy and procedures for proper accounting, documentation, and other record keeping activities required for the administration of clothing allowance and other issues.

3001. <u>SCOPE</u>. This policy and these procedures pertain to personnel of the Regular and Reserve establishment (unless otherwise specified). Additional procedures for Reserve personnel are provided in chapter 8 of this Manual. All clothing allowances and issues must be supported by a properly completed Combined Individual Clothing Requisition and Issue Slip form NAVMC 604 (men)/604B (women) and further documented on Individual Clothing Record form NAVMC 631 (men)/631A (women), per this chapter, unless otherwise indicated. Both forms may be downloaded from the Marine Corps Electronic Forms System (MCEFS) located at www.hqmc.usmc.mil/ar/recmgmt.nsf

3002. <u>FISCAL ACCOUNTING</u>

1. <u>HQMC Funding vs. Unit Funding</u>. Most personal clothing allowances and issues authorized by HQMC are funded using Military Personnel, Marine Corps (MILPERS) or Reserve MILPERS appropriations and require fulfillment of additional fiscal accounting activities. Other personal clothing issues may be directed locally by the unit/organization commander and are funded using local Operations and Maintenance, Marine Corps (O&MMC) appropriations.

    a. <u>HQMC Funded Allowances and Issues</u>. Authorized allowances and issues are currently assigned a Functional Account Number (FAN), per reference (q). FANs for clothing allowance issues are listed in figure 3-1 following. The FAN is provided on the NAVMC 604/604B, per paragraph 3003 following, and issues are typically made at an authorized MCSS/RCO, per figure 2-2 of this Manual. Reference (r) will provide a standard document number (SDN) and line of accounting (LOA) required for clothing purchases and reimbursement. A matrix table will be provided via the Bulletin

with the SDN/LOA that will be used by the clothing stores to
create the voucher to be submitted to DFAS for reimbursement.
Units/organizations that do not have access to a MCSS/RCO can
requisition items through the supply system using a MILSTRIP
document with the proper SDN/LOA and a signal code B.

        (1) Unit/Organization Responsibilities. The authorizing
unit/organization will provide all necessary issue information on
the NAVMC 604/604B, per paragraph 3003 following. Required
information includes the appropriate FAN, which identifies that
MILPERS appropriations should be used to fund the issue. Only
officers designated in writing by the commander may sign NAVMC
604/604Bs, as these forms authorize the expenditure of Government
funds.

        (2) MCSS/RCO Responsibilities. Currently, MCSS/RCOs must
provide a monthly FAN Report to CMC (RFM). Future fiscal
procedures to be provided in reference (r) will no longer require
the FAN report. Instead, an appropriate fiscal form will
annotate FAN level detail that will post to the accounting
system.

    b. Unit/Organization Funded Issues. Issues requiring O&MMC
funding must be funded using local O&MMC appropriations.
Units/organizations will either authorize issue via the NAVMC
604/604B at an MCSS/RCO or order clothing items via the supply
system, both per figure 2-2 of this Manual. However, when using
the NAVMC 604/604B for an O&MMC funded issue, complete unit
appropriation, including a full Standard Document Number
(SDN)/Line of Accounting (LOA), must be provided, per section
3003 following. Only officers may sign NAVMC 604/604Bs, as these
forms involve the direct expenditure of Government funds.

3003. DOCUMENTING ALLOWANCE AND OTHER ISSUES. Clothing
allowance and other issues must be documented on either a HQMC
approved local accounting form or a Combined Individual Clothing
Requisition and Issue Slip (form NAVMC 604/604B). A sample form
NAVMC 604B (Women's) is provided as figure 3-2. The NAVMC 604
(Men's) is identical to the NAVMC 604B (Women's), except for
different items lists.

1. Recruit Training Issues. In lieu of a NAVMC 604/604B for each individual recruit, a roster of all recruits to receive each phased clothing issue may be used by the MCRDs to support items issued. Recruits will sign a receipt to document all items issued.

   a. Separate rosters will be prepared by FY and active or reserve component to charges post to the correct MILPERS/Reserve MILPERS account. The current active duty date (date of last entry for active duty with the Marine Corps) and the names of each Marine will be entered on the appropriate roster.

   b. For each Marine who cannot be provided the complete initial issue, a mechanized due-member (DM) form must be inserted on top of the enlistment contract of the trasferring individual's SRB to bring attention to the gaining command of the required subsequent issuance, must be prepared. To ensure all initial issues are charged to the appropriation applicable at the time of entitlement, the words "CHARGE TO FY__ APPROPRIATION" will be annotated on the bottom margin of the DM form.

      (1) Appropriation data applicable at the time of entitlement will be reflected on the mechanized DM form. To ensure that all initial clothing allowance issues are charged to the appropriation applicable at the time of entitlement, the current active duty date (CURR ACDU) of the Marine will also be entered on the DM form. The forms will be prepared in an original only and will be headed "Due Individual to Complete Initial Issue." The form will be signed by the Depot Clothing Officer or another officer authorized in writing to approve such requisitions and will be inserted on the document side of the individual's SRB. Items not furnished because of the requirement for special order clothing will be indicated by the notation "SPEC ORDER" which will be shown next to the affected item.

      (2) If the amounts due the individual cannot be furnished completely by subsequent issue, the foregoing procedures will be repeated, ensuring that all data required is included on the DM form.

      (3) Commanders will ensure that the foregoing procedures are carefully followed, inasmuch as the mechanized DM form filed in the individual's SRB constitutes the only authority to make subsequent issues in fulfillment of the individual's Initial Issue at follow-on duty stations.

(4) All clothing that is due the individual, including special measurement clothing/footwear, that arrives after the individual has transferred from the MCRD, will be forwarded to the individual's new command for issue. The new command will complete the issue and the DM form and return it to the applicable MCRD. To alleviate delays in delivery of DM clothing and return of receipts required to support stores accounting records, the MCRD must notify the individual's new command to coordinate shipment and receipt. The subject items will be dropped from MCRD's inventory upon shipment and receipt of the completed DM form.

2. Officer Training Issues. Issues to candidates attending Officer Candidate School (OCS) will be documented on the NAVMC 604/604B and charged to the appropriate FAN.

    a. The original NAVMC 604/604B will be provided to OCS for inclusion in the individual's official military personnel file (OMPF). Enter in Block/Item 18 of the DD Form 214, "I understand that while I am serving my remaining reserve obligation for military service I am required to maintain all of my individual uniform clothing items for a minimum of 90 days from my discharge."

    b. A copy will be retained by the issuing officer.

    c. A copy will be furnished to the individual concerned.

3. Special Initial Clothing Allowance Issue to Navy Personnel. Issues to authorized Sailors are made at Field Medical School (FMS), typically via the local MCSS, and individual units per figure. 2-2 of this Manual. In lieu of a NAVMC 604/604B for each individual FMS student, the MCSS may use a roster of all students to support a Summary NAVMC 604/604B covering all students and all items issued. MCSSs will follow those instructions provided for bulk recruit issues, per paragraph 3003 preceding, substituting "Initial Clothing Allowance" with "Special Initial Clothing Allowance."

4. Cash Clothing Allowances. Cash clothing allowances are documented via unit diary entry and recorded in the members military pay account.

5. Supplementary Clothing Allowance and Other HQMC Funded Clothing Issues. Supplementary clothing allowance issues and other HQMC funded clothing issues will be documented on a NAVMC 604/604B.

    a. Unit/Organization Responsibilities. Commanders at the battalion/squadron or equivalent level for independent units/organizations will ensure the NAVMC 604/604B is completed properly before sending an authorized individual to a supporting MCSS/RCO to receive the allowance issue. Only officers designated in writing by the commander may sign NAVMC 604/604Bs, as these forms authorize the expenditure of Government funds. It is not the MCSS's responsibility to ensure that the correct allowance quantities are provided on the NAVMC 604/604B; this responsibility rests solely with the commander. Copies of individual's orders/web orders must be provided with the NAVMC 604/604B, to assist the MCSS/RCO with authorized issues. When an allowance issue is authorized for an activity not supported by an MCSS/RCO, the signed NAVMC 604/604B will be used to support a requisition through the supply system. The following sections on the NAVMC 604/604B must be completed:

        (1) Recipient name, grade, SSN, date of authorization, and current active duty date (date of last entry for active duty).

        (2) Authorized quantity (QTY) per item to be issued, per reference (c).

        (3) Type of issue (initial, supplementary, or replacement) and appropriate FAN.

        (4) Reference the paragraph number from this Manual, enclosure and page number from reference (c), or other HQMC/PMCUB authorization and T/O number or Responsible Unit Code (RUC), if applicable, which authorizes the allowance.

        (5) Complete unit address (unit office stamp with address is permitted).

        (6) Unit/organization Commanding Officer's (CO's) signature or signature of another officer authorized in writing to sign by-direction of the CO. Enlisted personnel are not authorized to sign correspondence that involves direct

expenditure of Government funds. This signature certifies that the requesting individual's record has been checked and the individual is authorized to the clothing allowance issue. A letter identifying officers authorized to sign the forms and their sample signatures must be provided to the supporting MCSS/RCO.

   (7) CO's or other authorized officer's printed name and rank.

   (8) Grade insignia, service stripes, trouser stripes, and waistplates may be issued in conjunction with supplementary clothing allowance issues and sewn on (if applicable) at Government expense under the specific circumstances described in paragraph 2009.1 preceding. However, a separate NAVMC 604/604B form with O&MMC appropriation must be provided to the MCSS/RCO. After the clothing is received and issue is made, a copy of the NAVMC 604/604B will be forwarded to the unit administrative section for appropriate documentation in the individual's official military personnel file (OMPF), per paragraph 3004 following.

   b. MCSS/RCO Responsibilities. MCSSs/RCOs retain a copy of the NAVMC 604/604B forms with accompanying financial voucher to support expenditure from the MILPERS and Reserve MILPERS appropriations. Copies may be maintained electronically (on diskette or CD) and should be retained for a minimum of 6 years and 3 months from date of issue. A copy will be forwarded to the individual's commander for retention in the individual's OMPF. The appropriate data from the NAVMC 604/604B will be transferred to a Public Voucher for Purchases and Services Other Than Personal (Standard Form (SF) 1034) for fiscal processing. The MCSS/RCO will require a separate NAVMC 604/604B form with O&MMC appropriation for authorized grade insignia, service stripes, trouser stripes, or waistplates, per paragraph 2009.1 of this Manual.

6. Unit/Organization Funded Clothing Issues

   a. Unit/Organization Responsibilities. Commanders at the battalion/squadron level or equivalent level for independent units/organizations will ensure the correct SDN/LOA/Tactical Address Code (TAC) combinations are provided on the NAVMC

604/604B, to identify the appropriate O&MMC fund to bill for the issue, per reference (q) or (r). Commanders will also ensure that the complete unit address is provided and that the form is signed, either by himself/herself or another officer authorized in writing to sign by-direction of the CO. Only officers designated in writing by the commander may sign NAVMC 604/604Bs, as these forms authorize the expenditure of Government funds. This signature certifies that the requesting individual's record has been checked and the individual is authorized to the clothing issue. The individual will then be issued the clothing by the unit or sent to the local MCSS/RCO for issue, per figure 2-2 of this Manual.

    b. MCSS/RCO Responsibilities. If a MCSS/RCO is used to make the O&MMC funded clothing issue, the store manager will verify that O&MMC appropriation data is provided on the NAVMC 604/604B and that the form is signed by the individual's CO, or other officer authorized in writing to sign by-direction of the CO, prior to making the issue. The O&MMC appropropriation data will be transferred to a form SF 1034 for fiscal processing. After issue action is completed, the signed NAVMC 604/604B will be used by the MCSS/RCO to support the requisition/issue.

3004. INDIVIDUAL CLOTHING RECORDS AND INVENTORIES. Clothing allowance and other clothing issues must be further documented on an Individual Clothing Record (form NAVMC 631 (Men's)/631A (Women's)) and maintained in the individual's OMPF, per reference (h). Other activities, including individual uniform clothing inventories, must also be documented on the NAVMC 631/631A. Responsibility for the preparation and maintenance of clothing records rests directly with the activity commander. However, details of administration may be delegated to appropriate assistants. Care shall be exercised by all personnel having official access to the records to prevent unauthorized entries. The Inspector General, Marine Corps (IGMC) inspects SRBs and OMPFs for proper maintenance of these forms. The NAVMC 631/631A may be downloaded from the MCEFS, per paragraph 3001 preceding. A sample form NAVMC 631 (Men's) is provided as figure 3-3. The NAVMC 631A (Women's) is identical to the NAVMC 604B (Men's), except for different items lists. Instructions for preparation and maintenance of Individual Clothing Records, forms NAVMC 631/631A, are as follows:

1. NAVMC 631/631A has been designed for use in both the Regular and Reserve Establishments. However, columns 1 through 4, inclusive, and certificate numbers 1 and 2 apply only to clothing furnished to personnel of the Marine Corps Reserve under the replacement in-kind process. Additional details for use by the Reserve Establishment are provided in chapter 8 of this Manual. Careful attention should be given to the columns and certificates to ascertain their applicability. An inventory and proper documentation on a NAVMC 631/631A is required for the following activities (in the columns and with the Certificates indicated):

    a. Issues to reservists, recalled retirees, and other individuals reporting for extended active duty (column 5, certificate 3), per chapter 9 of this Manual. When a Selected Marine Corps Reserve (SMCR) individual is ordered to extended active duty (more than 6 months of active duty), the SMCR activity commander will conduct a departing inventory, per paragraph 8009.5 of this Manual. Incoming inventories and issues to other other activated reservists will be conducted by the Mobilization Support Battalion (MSB) and/or Gaining Force Commander (GFC) per chapter 9 of this Manual.

    b. Supplementary clothing or special initial clothing allowance issues (column 6, certificate 4), per reference (c), and organizational issues of personal retention items (column 7, certificate 4), per chapter 7 of this Manual. If the individual does not have a NAVMC 631/631A at the time of issue, a new one will be established, per paragraph 3004.3 following. Indicate the type of issue (supplementary allowance, special initial clothing allowance, or personal retention item) under the appropriate column of the certificate. The duplicate form NAVMC 604/604B used to document the issue may be destroyed after the preceding entries have been made and verified. The NAVMC 631/631A must be maintained for a minimum of 3 years from the date of detachment from the organization where the issue occurred. Certificate 4 may also be used to document inventories of allowance or personal retention items on hand.

    c. Activities related to transfer to and from combat areas, as follows:

        (1) Clothing placed in storage at a clothing control point prior to transfer to a combat area (column 8, certificate 5), per paragraph 9004.1 of this Manual. A copy of the NAVMC

631/631A will be placed in the storage container. In the event that the clothing is received for storage at a point wherein it will require further transfer to a Personal Effects and Baggage Center (PEBC), the officer will so indicate on certificate 5, as follows:

"Received at (indicate organization). To be forwarded for storage at (indicate appropriate PEBC)."

(2) Clothing taken to a combat area, i.e. not placed in storage (column 9, certificate 5). Completion of these sections will provide data which might subsequently be required to effect replacement of such articles, when appropriate.

(3) Stored clothing returned to individuals upon arrival from a combat area, as required for further processing, either directly or via shipment (column 10, certificates 5A or 5B).

(4) Minimum Traveling Uniform issues made to individuals who are hospitalized or otherwise displaced from their clothing upon return from a combat area (column 11, certificate 4), per paragraph 9004.2 of this Manual.

d. Miscellaneous issues, to include Minimum Traveling Uniform issues to absentees, deserters, prisoners, hospitalized personnel (other than combat returnees), and issues for the burial of the dead (column 12, certificate 4). When issues are made to USMC absentees and deserters restored to a full duty status, the copy of the certificate will be made to support the supply officer's retained copy of the expenditure document used to expend the clothing so issued.

e. Recovery of uniforms for individuals discharged under the conditions cited in paragraph 6003 of this Manual (column 13).

f. Exit inventory and required counseling upon release from active duty or discharge (column 14, certificate 6), per paragraphs 3005.3 and 6002 of this Manual. Prior to effecting the release of an individual from active duty, unit/activity commanders must ensure that a clothing inventory is conducted and recorded and that the NAVMC 631/631A is forwarded with the SRB when an individual is released from active duty.

g. Miscellaneous activities such as replacement issues (i.e. Special Blue Uniform Replacement Allowance,) and other unique issues (column 15). This blank column is provided to allow for the incorporation of additional information as might be required. The recovery of unserviceable items to be replaced will be recorded in the blank space for column 15 (i.e., the title for column 15 will read "Recovered Supplementary Blues").

h. A NAVMC 631/631A is not required to show evidence of receipt of the Initial Issue at recruit training.

2. After entries to the NAVMC 631/631A have been made from a copy of a NAVMC 604/604B or a copy of the shipping document, the copies of the NAVMC 604/604B or the shipping document will be removed and destroyed.

3. In those cases when it becomes necessary to establish a new NAVMC 631/631A, such as any time a form is found to be missing or the form begins to appear illegible due to numerous entries or damage, a new inventory will be conducted. If any required items are found to be missing during the inventory, the commander will conduct an investigation to determine whether there is fault or negligence on the part of the individual for not maintaining the MRL of clothing. If a NAVMC 631/631A exists, all applicable information from previous supplementary allowance issues will be transferred to the new record.

3005. ADDITIONAL CLOTHING INSPECTIONS. Commanders shall make inspections at other times to ensure that personnel have in their possession all required items of individual uniform clothing and that these items are in a serviceable condition. Required items of individual uniform clothing are those which constitute the MRL, per chapter 4 of this Manual, plus any additional items issued as a supplementary or special initial clothing allowance and required to be possessed and maintained by the individual. Commanders shall direct the replacement of any required clothing found to be in an unserviceable condition. In addition to inspecting uniform clothing of individuals during the inventories detailed in paragraph 3004 preceding, inspections shall be conducted under the following circumstances:

1. Immediately Upon Attachment of an Individual.

2. At Periodic Intervals, for Fit and Condition, During the Individual's Assignment to the Organization.

    a. Commanders are responsible for the proper fit of uniform clothing on personnel under their command and shall ensure that all alterations, either at Government expense or at the expense of the individual, conform to the intent of these regulations and reference (i). The wearing of improperly fitted or altered uniform clothing is prohibited.

    b. Commanders shall give particular attention to recently graduated recruits immediately upon their attachment to their organizations to identify individuals who may have experienced profile changes to the extent that additional alterations of the service uniforms are required, per paragraph 2009.2.b of this Manual.

    c. Commanders from the MCRDs, OCS, and FMS shall designate representatives (male or female as appropriate) to act as witnessing officers for sales and issues to recruits, officer candidates, and students.

    d. It is recommended that Commanders conduct an annual seabag inspection for each individual, in conjunction with the anniversary month of his/her enlistment, to reinforce responsible management of the annual CRA payment.

3. Prior to Their Transfer From the Organization.

    a. Commanders shall ensure that individuals being transferred or discharged have in their possession all of the clothing items listed in the current MRL (per chapter 4 of this Manual) and any authorized supplementary clothing allowance issues (except as specified in paragraph 2008.1.a preceding), and that all such items are in a serviceable condition. Authorized supplementary clothing allowance issues would include all of those made during the current assignment and any previous assignment issues made within 3 years. In the event that an individual is being transferred from an overseas command not supported by an MCSS/RCO, this requirement may be waived until the individual reaches the new duty station.

b. Commanders shall ensure that all documents relating to supplementary clothing allowance issues are inserted on top of the enlistment contract of the transferring individual's SRB prior to transfer. In those cases where a complete issue was not made prior to transfer of the individual, insert a duplicate copy of the NAVMC 604/604B on top of the enlistment contract of the transferring individual's SRB, listing the items due the individual to complete the supplementary clothing allowance issue. The form will be removed upon arrival at the new unit so that remaining items may be issued.

FAN	ALLOWANCE	DESCRIPTION
72042	Initial Clothing Allowance (Male) (See paragraph 2003)	This FAN includes: • Initial Issues to male recruits. • Replacement issues for active duty male enlisted personnel for profile changes up to 6 months after reporting to the first permanent duty station. • Initial Issue to male enlisted musicians of the U.S. Marine Band. • Reduced Initial Issue to male reserve reenlistees. • Reduced Initial Issue to male commissioned officers or warrant officers (if applicable). • Reduced Initial Issue to unsuccessful male officer candidates assigned to further duty in an enlisted status. • Reduced Initial Issue to male prisoners restored to duty. This FAN does not include officer procurement programs (FAN 72049), female recruits or other initial female issues (FAN 72057), or Replacement Initial Clothing Issues/Minimum Combat Load (MCL) Issues to enlisted reserve personnel/other activated personnel on extended active duty (more than 6 months of active duty) (FAN 72060).
72043	Supplementary Clothing Allowance (Active Duty) (See paragraph 2008)	Extra clothing allowances, per reference (c). This FAN includes: • Blue dress uniform allowance issues and replacement blue uniform allowance issues (specific MOS's only). • Utility uniform allowance issues. • Maternity uniform issues. • Other miscellaneous supplementary uniform issues to authorized enlisted personnel. Since all issues of this type cannot be provided a separate FAN for reporting purposes, those issues that are otherwise authorized, but are not specifically described in paragraph 2008, will be identified with this FAN.
72047	Special Initial Clothing Allowances to Enlisted Navy Personnel (See paragraph 2004)	Initial Issues to Navy personnel serving with Marine Corps units. This FAN includes: • Special Initial Utility Uniform Allowance (SIUUA) • Special Initial Service Uniform Allowance (SISUA) to both active duty and reserve Enlisted Navy personnel serving with Marine Corps units.

Figure 3-1.--Clothing Allowance Functional Account Numbers (FANs).

INDIVIDUAL CLOTHING REGULATIONS

FAN	ALLOWANCE	DESCRIPTION
72048	Miscellaneous Issues/Replacements Issues (See paragraph 2009 and Chapter 6)	This FAN includes: • Replacements issues to combat returnees (to include POW's). • Replacements issues to hospitalized personnel. • Replacement issues for the burial of the dead. • Claims authorized by the Personal Property Claims Regulations of the JAG Manual. • Replacements issues to absentees and deserters restored to full time duty. • Replacements issues to prisoners. • Other miscellaneous issues, as required.
72049	Initial Clothing Allowances for Officer Programs (See paragraph 2005)	This FAN includes: • Platoon Leader's Class (PLC). • Officer Candidates Course (OCC). • Enlisted commissioning programs (active and reserve). • NROTC Marine-Option. • Service academy training at Officer Candidates School (OCS). For both men and women.
72053	Replacement Issues Incident to Military Service in a Combat Area (See Chapter 9)	This FAN includes replacement issues for clothing items destroyed, damaged, lost, abandoned, captured, or otherwise rendered unusable incident to military service in a combat area, if the loss was not caused by any fault or negligence of the member. The unit's MSC commander must approve the issues and sign the NAVMC 604/604B.
72057	Initial Clothing Allowance (Female) (See paragraph 2003)	This FAN includes the same issues as detailed in FAN 72042, except this FAN is to be used only for females. This FAN does not include officer procurement programs (FAN 72049) or Replacement Initial Clothing Issues/Minimum Combat Load (MCL) Issues to enlisted reserve personnel/other activated personnel on extended active Duty (more than 6 months of active duty) (FAN 72060).

Figure 3-1.--Clothing Allowance Functional Account Numbers (FANs)— continued.

3-16

FAN	ALLOWANCE	DESCRIPTION
72060	Replacement Initial Clothing Issues or Minimum Combat Load Issues to Mobilized Enlisted Reservists and other Activated Personnel on Extended Active Duty (more than 6 months of active duty) (both male and female) (See Chapter 9)	This FAN includes replacement issues to authorized activated personnel, including civilians serving with Marine Corps units.

Figure 3-1.--Clothing Allowance Functional Account Numbers
(FANs)— continued.

COMBINED INDIVIDUAL CLOTHING REQUISTION AND ISSUE SLIP (WOMEN'S) (10120)
NAVMC 604B Rev. 08-03 (EF) (Previous editions are obsolete and will not be used)
SN: 0109-LF-986-7300

NAME (Last, First, Middle Initial) Marine, Always A.		GRADE E-3	SSN 123-45-6789	DATE 20050426

IT IS REQUESTED THAT THE BELOW LISTED ARTICLES BE FURNISHED FOR MY PERSONAL USE.
SIGNATURE: *A A Marine*

CURR ACDU (Date of last entry for active duty) 20040403

SIZE	ITEM	QTY	UNIT PRICE	TOTAL PRICE	SIZE	ITEM	QTY	UNIT PRICE	TOTAL PRICE
	BAG, DUFFEL, w/carrying strap								
	BELT, MARTIAL ARTS, color								
						BLUE UNIFORM ISSUES			
	CAP, DRESS: white, vinyl				7	CAP, DRESS: white, vinyl	1	$62.15	$62.15
					ML	COAT, WOMAN'S: all-season poly/wool gabardine, blue	1	$105.80	$105.80
					6	GLOVES: cloth, white, pair	2	$6.60	$13.20
					—	INSIGNIA, BOS: collar, gold plated, pair	1	$1.95	$1.95
					M	NECK TAB, WOMAN'S: black	1	$5.15	$5.15
					32	SHIRT, WOMAN'S: white	2	$10.80	$21.60
					32	SKIRT, WOMAN'S: all-season poly/wool gabardine, blue	1	$27.05	$27.05
					32	SLACKS, WOMAN'S: all-season poly/wool gabardine, blue, pair	2	$28.95	$57.90

TOTAL ISSUE $294.80

APPROVED: The individual named hereon is authorized to draw the clothing requested under the type issue indicated:

		FAN:
	INITIAL ISSUE	
X	SUPPLEMENTARY ISSUE	72043
	REPLACEMENT ISSUE	
	CHECKAGE SALE	

REFERENCE MCBul 10120, FY06, Encl (6), T/O No. 5014, Med Blue
1st Bn, 6th Marines 2d MarDiv Camp Lejeune, NC 28542
(Insert office stamp of issuing office)

DATE 04/27/05

I ACKNOWLEDGE receipt of articles of clothing indicated above and accept these items as fitting properly, or appropriate alterations have been prescribed. SIGNATURE: *A A Marine*

I hereby CONSENT to checkage of my pay account in the amount indicated under total issue. SIGNATURE:

I CERTIFY that I have witnessed the issue of the clothing enumerated above and that issues have been made in the manner indicated. Outer articles of clothing issued are the proper size, or appropriate alterations have been prescribed. *I C Store*
Witnessing Signature (when required)

O&MMC FUNDED ISSUE UNIT APPROPRIATION DATA
I T Commander ,U.S.M.C.
(COMMANDING OFFICER'S SIGNATURE)
Iam T. Commander, LtCol, USMC
(COMMANDING OFFICER'S PRINTED NAME & RANK)

Figure 3-2.—Sample Form NAVMC 604B.

INDIVIDUAL CLOTHING RECORD (MEN'S) (10120)
NAVMC 631 (Rev 11-04) (EF) (Previous edition are obsolete and will not be used)
SN: 0109-LF-130-4000

NAME (Last) (First) (Middle Initial)		GRADE	SSN										
Hardcharger, James T.		E-4	123-45-7777										

Form must be maintained in individual's Service Record Book
*Refer to MCO P10120.28, MCO P4050.38, and MCO P4400.150 for instructions on using this form.

ITEMS	1 ON HAND	2 ISSUES	3 ISSUES	4 RECOVERY	5 REPORTING FOR ACTIVE DUTY ISSUES (CERT 3)	6 SUPPLEMENTARY ITEMS (CERT 4)	7 PERSONAL RETENTION ITEMS (CERT 4)	8 ITEMS STORED (CERT 5)	9 ITEMS TAKEN TO COMBAT (CERT 5)	10 ITEMS RETURNED TO MEMBER (CERT 5A OR 5B)	11 MINIMUM TRAVELING UNIFORM ISSUE (FROM COMBAT AREA) (CERT 4)	12 MISCELLANEOUS ISSUES (CERT 4)	13 CLOTHING RECOVERED	14 EXIT INVENTORY (CERT 6)	15 Recovered Supplementary Blues
DATE					2/1/05	12/4	1/15	2/2/05	2/4/05	7/15/05				1/7/05 12/1/04	
BAG, DUFFEL: w/carrying strap								1	1	1				2	
BELT, COAT, MAN'S: cotton, white					1			1	1	1				2	
BELT, MARTIAL ARTS: color:								2						1	
BELT, REFLECTIVE, SAFETY								1	2	1				3	
BELT, TROUSERS: web, khaki								4						4	
BOOTS, MARINE CORPS COMBAT: temperate weather, olive mohave, pair					1			2						2	
BOOTS, MARINE CORPS COMBAT: hot weather, olive mohave, pair					1			2						2	
BUCKLE: f/belt (coat)						1			1					1	
BUCKLE: f/belt, web, khaki								2						2	
CAP, COMBAT UTILITY: field, desert MARPAT								2						2	
CAP, COMBAT UTILITY: field, woodland MARPAT								2						2	
CAP, COMBAT UTILITY: garrison, desert MARPAT								2						1	
CAP, COMBAT UTILITY: garrison, woodland MARPAT								1						1	
CAP, COMBAT, woodland camouflage pattern								1							
CAP, GARRISON, MAN'S: all-season polyester/wool gabardine, green								2		2				2	
CLASP, NECKTIE								2		2				2	
COAT, COMBAT UTILITY: desert MARPAT								2						2	
COAT, COMBAT UTILITY: woodland MARPAT								2						2	
COAT, MAN'S: all-season, polyester/wool, gabardine, green, w/belt							1			1				2	
COAT, MAN'S: all-weather							1							1	
COAT, MAN'S: all-season, polyester/wool, gabardine, blue					1		1			1				1	1
CROWN SERVICE CAP: all-season, polyester/wool, gabardine, green							1			1				1	
CROWN SERVICE CAP: polyester/rayon, white					1		1			1				1	
DRAWERS, MAN'S: cotton, white, pair								6						6	
FRAME, SERVICE CAP					1		1			1				1	
GLOVES: cloth, white, pair					2		2			2				2	1
GLOVES: leather, black, pair							1		1					1	
INSIGNIA, BRANCH OF SERVICE: collar, gold-plated, pair					1		1			1				1	
INSIGNIA, BRANCH OF SERVICE: dress cap, gold-plated, screwpost							1			1				1	
INSIGNIA, BRANCH OF SERVICE: garrison cap, black, screwpost							1			1				1	
INSIGNIA, BRANCH OF SERVICE: service cap, black, screwpost							1			1				1	
INSIGNIA, BRANCH OF SERVICE: service uniform collar, black, pair							1			2				1	
INSIGNIA, BUTTON: dress cap, gold-plated							1			1				2	
INSIGNIA, BUTTON: service cap, black							1			1				1	
INSIGNIA, GRADE, ENLISTED PERSONNEL: green on khaki, pair							1							1	
INSIGNIA, GRADE, ENLISTED PERSONNEL: green on scarlet, pair															
INSIGNIA, GRADE, ENLISTED PERSONNEL: plastic, black, pair)								2	2	2				4	
NAME & SERVICE TAPE: embroidered desert MARPAT, f/combat coat & trousers (set of 3)								2						2	
NAME & SERVICE TAPE: embroidered woodland MARPAT, f/combat coat & trousers (set of 3)								2						2	
NECKTIE, KHAKI								2		2				2	
SHIRT, MAN'S: polyester/wool, khaki, long-sleeve								2		2				2	
SHIRT, MAN'S: polyester/wool, khaki, quarter-length-sleeve								2		2				2	
SHOE, DRESS: black, pair								2		2				2	
SOCKS: boot, pair								6						6	
SOCKS: dress, black, pair								4	2	4				6	
SOCKS WHITE, ATHLETIC (3 pair package)								4						4	
STRIPE, TROUSERS (NCO): scarlet, pair								2		2				2	
STRIPE, SERVICE: green on scarlet, pair															
SWEAT PANTS: green w/insignia, pair							1			1				1	
SWEAT SHIRT: green w/insignia							1			1				1	
SWEATER: pull-over, olive green, w/epaulettes							1			1				1	
TROUSERS, COMBAT UTILITY: desert MARPAT, pair								2						2	
TROUSERS, COMBAT UTILITY: woodland MARPAT, pair								2						2	
TROUSERS, MAN'S: all-season, polyester/wool gabardine, green, pair								2		2				2	
TROUSERS, MAN'S: all-season, polyester/wool gabardine, blue, pair					2			2		2				2	1
TRUNKS, GENERAL PURPOSE: nylon, olive green, pair								4						4	
UNDERSHIRT, MAN'S: cotton, white, crew-neck								6						6	
UNDERSHIRT: cotton, green								6						6	
WAISTPLATE: insignia (SNCOs only)															
WAISTPLATE: insignia w/o wreath (NCOs only)							1			1				1	
WAISTPLATE: plain (lance corporal and below only)						1									
Trunk, Locker						1								1	
Boots, Safety						1								1	

Designed using FormFlow 2.23, HQMC/ARDE, Oct 93

Figure 3-3.——Sample Form NAVMC 631.

NAVMC 631 (REV. 11-04) (EF) (BACK)

CERTIFICATE NO. 1

(CERTIFICATE TO BE USED BY SELECTED MARINE CORPS RESERVE UNITS)

I CERTIFY that the issue, recovery, inventory, or combination thereof, as attested to by me below, was made in the amounts or with the results indicated: (Duplicate NAVMC 604 form supporting the issue has been destroyed.)

DATE MADE	ORGANIZATION WHERE MADE	ISSUE PER COL. NO.	RECOV-ERY PER COL.	ON HAND PER COL.	ATTESTED TO BY	DATE ATTESTED

CERTIFICATE NO. 2

(CERTIFICATE TO BE USED BY SMCR UNITS FOR INVENTORY PRIOR TO TRANSFER OF MEMBER TO EXTENDED ACTIVE DUTY)

ORGANIZATION _____

I CERTIFY that the quantities indicated in column 1 are on hand prior to transfer of subject member to extended active duty.

_____ DATE _____
(Inventory officer's signature)

CERTIFICATE NO. 3

(CERTIFICATE FOR ISSUE MADE MEMBER OF MCR UPON REPORTING FOR EXTENDED ACTIVE DUTY)

ORGANIZATION   Mobilization Support Battalion, Camp Lejeune, NC

I CERTIFY that the issue listed in column 5 was made on indicated date, bringing total of clothing in possession of subject member to current prescribed minimum allowance for personnel on active duty: (Duplicate NAVMC 604 form supporting the issue has been destroyed.)

M. L. Charge   DATE   02012005
(Witnessing officer's signature)

CERTIFICATE NO.4

(CERTIFICATE REGARDING ISSUE/INVENTORY MADE)

I CERTIFY that the issue or inventory (columns 6 and/or 7) or combination thereof, as attested to by below was duly made in the amounts or with the results indicated: (Duplicate NAVMC 604 form supporting the issue has been destroyed)

DATE MADE	ORGANIZATION WHERE MADE	ISSUE PER COLUMN NUMBER (6or 7)	ON HAND PER COLUMN NUMBER	ISSUE TYPE	ATTESTED TO BY	DATE ATTESTED
	1st Battalion, 6th Marines		7		R.B. Over	11/15/04
12/4/04	MCAS Cherry Point, NC	6		Sup Blue (M)	LM Boss	12/4/04

(CERTIFICATES REGARDING CLOTHING STORAGE DATA)

Date Inventoried and Stored   2/2/05   Stored At   PEBC Cherry Point, NC

CERTIFICATE NO. 5

INVENTORY AND STORAGE:

I CERTIFY that quantities of clothing indicated in column 8 represent actual amounts of clothing inventoried by me and stored as indicated above. Items taken with me to combat are indicated in column 9.

ATTEST: _J.F. Hardcharger_   _M.O. Nottingham_   DATE   2/2/05
(Member's Signature)   (Inventory Officer's Signature)

RECEIVED AT: 2nd Battalion, 2nd Marines   TO BE FORWARDED FOR STORAGE AT: Cherry Point, NC
(Indicate Organization)   (Indicate PEBC)

CERTIFICATE NO. 5A

RETURN DIRECT TO MEMBER:

I CERTIFY that I have this date received the articles of clothing indicated in column 10 in the same quantity and condition as they were in when placed in storage: (Issue per column made to compensate for discrepancies discovered) or (See NAVMC 604 attached for items due member).

ATTEST: _J.F. Hardcharger_   _M.M. Smith_   DATE   7/15/05
(Member's Signature)   (Witnessing Officer's Signature)

CERTIFICATE NO. 5 B

SHIPPED TO MEMBER:

I CERTIFY that the clothing listed in column10 was shipped this date, at Government expense, to:

CONSIGNEE _____

ADDRESS _____

_____ DATE _____
(Cognizant Supply Officer's signature)

CERTIFICATE NO. 6

(CERTIFICATE UPON RELEASE FROM ACTIVE DUTY AND/OR DISCHARGE)

I UNDERSTAND that I am required to bring with me all individual uniform clothing items in my possession (Indicated in column 14) upon release from active duty if I am ever activated while still under contract or within 90 days of complete discharge.

J.F. Hardcharger   DATE   01/17/05
(Member's signature)

Figure 3-3.--Sample Form NAVMC 631 - continued.

INDIVIDUAL CLOTHING REGULATIONS

CHAPTER 4

MINIMUM REQUIREMENTS

CHAPTER 4

MINIMUM REQUIREMENTS

4000. <u>INTRODUCTION</u>. A Minimum Requirements List (MRL) is a listing, by item and quantity, of individual uniform clothing that enlisted personnel must have in their possession and maintain in a serviceable condition.

4001. <u>SCOPE</u>. These requirements pertain to enlisted Marines of the Regular and Reserve establishment and enlisted Sailors issued a special initial uniform allowance, per paragraph 2004 of this Manual. Minimum requirements for officers are provided in reference (d).

4002. <u>PUBLICATION</u>. Updated MRLs are published annually, at the beginning of each Fiscal Year (FY), in reference (c).

4003. <u>REGULATIONS</u>. These regulations specifically prohibit enlisted personnel from being required to possess clothing in excess of the MRL. Personnel are permitted to purchase additional items above the MRL at their own expense, but may not be directed to do so by their superiors.

1. <u>Recruit Initial Clothing Allowance Issue</u>. While undergoing recruit training, enlisted personnel will be required to maintain a minimum allowance of individual uniform clothing provided as an Initial Issue, per paragraph 2003 of this Manual.

2. <u>Mandatory Possession Dates</u>. Mandatory possession dates are established for enlisted Marines and Sailors to possess new clothing items or revised quantities, per reference (c). New items not issued with an initial clothing allowance or via a gratuitous issue will not be added to the MRL and assigned a mandatory possession date until CRA is adjusted and sufficient time has been provided to accrue funds to purchase the new items.

3. <u>Optional Items</u>. Amplifying notes to MRLs explain circumstances that permit personnel to have in their possession items other than those listed. Per references (c) and (d),

personnel are authorized to buy, as optional replacements to meet MRLs, approved commercial uniform items that in some cases are of higher quality than those initially issued. These optional uniform items are often more expensive than the issued uniform items. Personnel cannot be directed to purchase optional commercial uniform items.

4.   During Temporary Additional Duty (TAD). When personnel are assigned to TAD and return to the parent organization is contemplated upon completion of such TAD, the individual is only required to take those quantities and types of clothing expected to be utilized in performing TAD. Clothing not taken by the individual will be stored at the parent organization per the provisions of reference (s), unless the individual is residing in other quarters.

INDIVIDUAL CLOTHING REGULATIONS

CHAPTER 5

SOURCES OF SUPPLY

<table>
<tr><td></td><td><u>PARAGRAPH</u></td><td><u>PAGE</u></td></tr>
<tr><td>INTRODUCTION...............................</td><td>5000</td><td>5-3</td></tr>
<tr><td>SCOPE......................................</td><td>5001</td><td>5-3</td></tr>
<tr><td>BACKGROUND.................................</td><td>5002</td><td>5-3</td></tr>
<tr><td>SOURCES OF SUPPLY..........................</td><td>5003</td><td>5-4</td></tr>
<tr><td>SOURCE OF SUPPLY RESPONSIBILITIES AND
SPECIAL CIRCUMSTANCES......................</td><td>5004</td><td>5-11</td></tr>
<tr><td>ADDITIONAL MILITARY CLOTHING SALES STORE
(MCSS)AND SUPPORTED INSTALLATION
RESPONSIBILITIES...........................</td><td>5005</td><td>5-18</td></tr>
</table>

CHAPTER 5

SOURCES OF SUPPLY

5000. INTRODUCTION. This chapter provides information on the authorized sources of supply for uniform clothing, to include organizations and retail stores that issue and/or sell uniform clothing items. It also describes responsibilities for each source of supply.

5001. SCOPE. This policy and these procedures apply to authorized organizations that provide uniform clothing or clothing support services to Marines and Sailors serving with Marines. Additional contracts and agreements, with sources of supply external to the Marine Corps, apply.

5002. BACKGROUND. There are two types of uniform clothing items made available through authorized sources of supply for issue or sale to authorized personnel:

- Marine Corps Supply "System" Items
- Commercial "Non-System" Items

1. Supply System Items. Supply system items are those items available for requisition through the Marine Corps authorized supply system for sale or issue at Fiscal Year (FY) established prices with no price mark-up. System items can either sold or issued to authorized personnel and include initial clothing allowance (seabag) issues and supplementary clothing allowance issues. Prices are established annually by DSCP or another HQMC authorized provider.

2. Commercial Non-System Items. Commercial non-system items are those items procured from commercial sources outside of the Marine Corps supply system for sale at a profit, i.e. at marked-up prices, per paragraph 5003.2 of this Manual. Commercial non-system items include optional items (per the references (c) and (d), officer uniform items, and required uniform items that are not available through the supply system (i.e., certain personal items, shoes, etc.). For those required items that are not available through the system, a cash clothing allowance is provided per paragraph 2007 of this Manual.

5003. SOURCES OF SUPPLY. Authorized system and non-system uniform clothing items may be obtained from any of the following sources:

* Retail Clothing Outlet (RCO)
* Marine Corps Community Services Exchange (MCX) Military Clothing Sales Store (MCSS)
* Navy Exchange Service Command (NEXCOM)
* Army and Air Force Exchange Service (AAFES)
* Using Unit (via DSCP or other HQMC authorized provider)

1. Retail Clothing Outlet (RCO). RCOs, also known as "cash sales" stores, sell or issue only supply system items. The stockage of optional uniform items is not authorized.

    a. There are two RCOs remaining in the Marine Corps and they function primarily to provide initial issue of clothing to inductees:

        (1) RCO Quantico, VA. RCO Quantico (Supplementary Address Code MMQU18) manages initial issues to candidates attending Officer Candidates School (OCS) and personnel deploying as part of the MSGBn.

        (2) RCO Marine Corps Recruit Depot (MCRD) San Diego, CA. RCO San Diego (Supplementary Address Code MMSU10) manages initial issues to recruits. This RCO is authorized to accept recruit debit cards or other approved forms of payment controlled by the local MCX.

    b. Stock permitting, RCOs can also sell system items to individuals. All RCO sales are done by cash or check; credit cards are not accepted. Checkage sales are also authorized when purchase by cash sales would create a personal hardship, as certified by the individual's commanding officer on a NAVMC 604/604B, per paragraph 5004 following.

    c. RCOs are responsible for maintaining stock and inventory records, making issues/sales to authorized customers, and reporting transactions to the Commanding General, Marine Corps Logistics Command (CG, MARCORLOGCOM). Replenishment of RCO clothing stocks will be accomplished by submitting MILSTRIP requisitions to DSCP or other HQMC authorized source of supply.

d. Organizations supported by a RCO may use Operations and Maintenance, Marine Corps (O&MMC) funds via O&MMC appropriation data to requisition system items in bulk for issue to authorized personnel.

e. Additional responsibilities for alterations are provided in paragraph 2009.2 and for disposition of recovered clothing are provided in paragraph 6004 of this Manual.

2. Marine Corps Community Services Exchange (MCX) Military Clothing Sales Store (MCSS). In 1981, the United States Congress directed that the three exchange systems (MCX, NEXCOM, and AAFES) take over the uniform clothing cash sales functions for the services. MCSSs operated by Marine Corps Community Services Exchanges (MCXs) perform these functions at most Marine Corps bases and stations. The Personal and Family Readiness Division, M&RA Deparment, Headquarters Marine Corps, Quantico, Viriginia (CMC (MR)) oversees the MCCS operation, management, and supervision of all Marine Corps MCSS facilities, excluding those in Okinawa, which are operated and managed by AAFES, per pargraph 5003.4 folowing. CMC (MR) also provides oversight to the MCCS mail-order program provided by the Navy Uniform Support Center, Chesapeake, VA, per paragraph 5003.3 following.

a. Military Clothing Sales Store (MCSS). MCSS facilities are authorized to stock and sell supply system uniform clothing, commercially procured non-system military uniform items to support the mission of the installation, and individual combat clothing and equipment (ICCE), in accordance with specific guidance provided by DC, I&L. MCSS facilities may also stock and sell, space permitting, non-related military logo items that enhance morale and esprit de corps.

(1) MCSSs are established at each of the following bases and stations:

- Henderson Hall, HQMC, Washington D.C.
- Marine Corps Air Ground Combat Center (MCAGCC) 29 Palms, CA
- Marine Corps Air Station (MCAS) Beaufort, SC
- MCAS Cherry Point, NC
- MCAS Iwakuni, Japan
- MCAS Miramar, CA
- MCAS Yuma, AZ

5003 INDIVIDUAL CLOTHING REGULATIONS

- Marine Corps Base (MCB) Camp Allen, Norfolk, VA
- MCB Camp Lejeune, NC
- MCB Camp Pendleton, CA
- MCB Kaneohe Bay, HI
- Marine Corps Logistics Base (MCLB) Albany, GA
- MCLB Barstow, CA
- MCRD Parris Island, SC

(2) Organizations supported by a MCSS may requisition system items for issue to authorized personnel.

(3) Additional responsibilities for alterations are provided in paragraph 2009.2 and for disposition of recovered clothing are provided in paragraph 6004 of this Manual.

(4) See paragraphs 5004 and 5005 following for additional details on MCSSs.

b. Central Stocking Points for Commercial Clothing Items. Many MCSS operations share sales areas with other MCX activities that sell CG, MARCORSYSCOM approved commercial non-system uniform items. The central stocking points for commercial uniform clothing items are The Basic School Uniform Shop at Camp Barrett, MCB Quantico, VA for male and female items and the MCXs at MCB Camp Lejeune and MCB Camp Pendleton for male only items.

(1) The depth of stock and selection of commercially procured items at these central stocking points are designed to provide full support to Marines throughout the Marine Corps through direct purchase, individual mail order, or special orders placed through other MCX resale operations. The desired goal is a service level of 95 percent.

(2) Other MCX resale operations may purchase commercial uniform clothing items from these central stocking points or directly from CG, MARCORSYSCOM approved sources, and shall likewise provide a balanced stock assortment of uniform clothing items in sufficient quantity to satisfy local demand.

(3) Uniform clothing items transferred between central stocking points will be transferred at the established price plus shipping charges indicated on the invoice.

(4) Items provided to other MCXs or to individuals from
the Central Stocking Points in support of special orders/mail-
orders will be at regular prices less the alteration charge,
whenever applicable.

c. <u>Pricing for Commercial Non-System Clothing Items</u>. The
sales prices for commercially procured uniform clothing items
shall be established by the local MCCS Director, per the
following guidelines:

(1) Commercially procured uniform clothing items should
be merchandized in the same manner as other merchandise and
should be marked up in an amount sufficient to recover all costs,
including a proportionate share of general overhead expenses, and
to generate a profit in direct relationship to other similar
merchandise.

(2) The cost of freight should be considered when
establishing an appropriate markup and, when separately stated
freight charges are included on the invoice, these separately
stated charges will not be added to the sales price.

(3) The markup established for those uniform clothing
items normally requiring alteration should be sufficient to cover
average cost of alteration required for initial fit and no
additional charges are authorized. Additional markup to cover
the cost of alterations is not appropriate if alteration service
is not, in fact, available to the customer.

(4) MCXs designated to stock and sell various uniform
clothing items are expected to maintain a balanced stock
assortment. Therefore, special handling charges for odd or
unusual sizes and less than minimum shipments will not be
included in the sales price except to the extent that they impact
on the overall cost of doing business and the standard markup is
applied.

d. <u>Customer Service Support for Commercial Non-System
Clothing Items</u>. MCX managers must cooperate fully with each
other to ensure maximum support in providing Marines and Sailors
with their required uniforms.

(1) MCXs not designated as central stocking points will
establish a customer service program to assist all individuals in

procuring required uniform clothing items. This program will include, but is not limited to, an inter-exchange uniform special order program with appropriate signs, handouts with instructions for special order uniform measurement and alteration services (only for commercially procured uniform clothing items).

       (a) Mail-order sales shall be treated by the shipping MCX as a regular sale, except when the mail order includes items that have been marked up to include alterations, in which case the invoice will reflect the original sales price of the item less the markup for which alterations have not been provided.

       (b) Uniform clothing items sent either directly to individuals or MCXs in support of the mail-order program are not eligible for parcel post shipment with postage and fees paid by the Government. Shipping charges shall be added and shown on the invoice.

       (c) For inter-exchange uniform clothing special orders, the receiving MCX shall treat the sale as a sale at cost and will not pay regular and central construction fund assessments. Under these conditions, the uniform sale is eligible for the Uniform Clothing Deferred Payment Plan (UCDPP) in existence at the receiving command.

       (2) The UCDPP authorizes the sale of commercial uniform clothing items to officers, staff noncommissioned officers, chief petty officers, petty officers first class, and to officer candidates on a deferred payment plan in accordance with locally prescribed standard operating procedures (SOPs). In view of the central stocking point concept for uniform clothing, it is essential that those commands designated as central stocking points expand their UCDPP to include personnel in the aforementioned categories, regardless of where they are stationed.

3. NEXCOM. Marines may purchase uniform clothing from a supporting NEXCOM military clothing sales store and will receive the same quality service as is provided to Navy customers. Marines may also receive authorized clothing allowance issues through NEXCOM's Uniform Support Center in Chesapeake, VA, as detailed below. NEXCOM also manages mail-order sales for the MCCS.

a. Types of Mail-Order Sales/Issues. NEXCOM accepts mail, phone, electronic mail (email), and on-line orders twenty-four-hours-a-day, 7-days-a-week. Ordering methods are as follows:

(1) In-Store Ordering. For special orders and authorized clothing allowance issues via a NEXCOM store, customers must use one of the red direct-order phones located in each NEXCOM facility and ask for the Government Accounts Team. A NAVMC 604/604B must be faxed to the NEXCOM Uniform Support Center (Attn: Government Accounts Team), at FAX # (757) 420-5675/5742. If necessary, special measurements can be taken at the NEXCOM store. However, the NEXCOM store will not complete the issue, as this must be done via the NEXCOM Uniform Support Center.

(2) Mail Ordering. Orders may be placed by mail to:

Uniform Support Center
Mail-Order Program
1545 Crossways Blvd, Suite 200
Chesapeake, VA 23320

Orders to fill an authorized clothing allowance issue must be made to the attention of the Government Accounts Team and must include a copy of the completed and certified NAVMC 604/604B.

(3) Telephone Ordering. Orders may be placed, toll free, using the following telephone numbers:

- Continental United States, Hawaii, Virgin Islands, and Puerto Rico, Quam, 1-800-368-4088
- Local Virginia 1-757-420-7348
- Alaska 1-800-368-4089
- Bahrain 800-477
- Canada 1-800-231-6289
- Germany 0800-82-93420
- Italy 8008-72441
- Japan 00531-11-4026
- Singapore 800-1100-198
- South Korea 008-1-800-958-8272
- Spain 900-98-1292
- United Kingdom 0800-89-4372
- Overseas DSN 312-253-8494

Telephone orders to fill an authorized authorized clothing allowance issue must be made to the attention of the Government Accounts Team by selecting option "7" during the call; a certified NAVMC 604/604B must also be faxed to the attention of Government Accounts at (757) 420-5675/5742.

        (4) E-Mail Ordering. Orders may be placed via e-mail to USCUSTOMERSERVICE@NEXNET.NAVY.MIL. Clothing allowance issues cannot be processed via e-mail.

        (5) On-Line Ordering. Orders may be placed on-line via the MCCS On-Line Uniform Store at http://www.usmc-mccs.org/uniforms/index.htm. In addition to a complete line of enlisted USMC uniforms, the website also provides for limited sales of Officer uniform clothing and other commercial non-system uniform clothing. Clothing Allowance issues cannot be processed on-line.

    b. Information for Mail-Order Sales. The following information is required when placing an order with the Uniform Support Center:

Name (Last, First, MI)	Rank or Rate
Social Security Number/	Gender
Service Number	Contact Number
Copy of DD214 (retirees or	Item(s) Desired
eligible veterans)	Quantity
Birthdate	Shipping Address

    c. Payment Methods. Payment may be made by credit card (Visa, Master Card, Discover, American Express) or the retail portion of the Military Star Card (Uniform Deferred Payment Program not accepted) or remitted upon receipt of the invoice, enclosed with the shipment.

    d. Shipment. All orders will be shipped within 24 hours. INCONUS customers should receive their orders in 7-10 working days (depending on carrier controls). Overnight air shipment is available upon request for an additional shipping charge.

4. Army and Air Force Exchange Service (AAFES). AAFES manages Marine Corps MCSSs in Okinawa and also provides for walk-in sales at their retail store locations. A Memorandum of Agreement between AAFES and CG, MARCORLOGCOM dictates the policies and procedures for the operation of these stores.

5. Using Unit. Commands not serviced by one of the above listed retail stores, including the MCRD initial issue points, will requisition authorized clothing issue items from Defense Supply Center, Philadelphia (DSCP) or another HQMC authorized provider. Requisitions may be processed by MILSTRIP requisition or via the DSCP website at http://ct.dscp.dla.mil/ascot/index.html.

5004. SOURCE OF SUPPLY RESPONSIBILITIES AND SPECIAL CIRCUMSTANCES. This paragraph details the following clothing source of supply responsibilities and instructions for handling special circumstances:

- Quality Assurance (Supply Deficiency Reports and Product Quality Deficiency Reports)
- Checkage Sales
- Special Measurement Orders
- Not in Stock (NIS)
- Sales to Other Than Regular or Reserve Marines or Sailors

1. Quality Assurance (QA). Initial QA is performed by DSCP or other authorized third party logistics provider. The source of supply should perform secondary QA upon receipt and at the point of issue/sale. The following procedures must be followed when discrepancies exist, either in quantity or quality:

   a. Supply Deficiency Report (SDR). Upon receipt of uniform supply system clothing and accessory items which do not match the receipt, a SDR should be submitted to:

   CG, MARCORLOGCOM
   Supply Chain Management Center
   Customer Relationship Management (Code 580A)
   814 Radford Blvd, Albany GA 31704-0320

   DSN 567-6765/66/67
   1-800-952-3352
   FAX DSN 567-5498
   email: SDRsRODs@logcom.usmc.mil

   b. Product Quality Deficiency Report (PQDR). Upon receipt
of supply system uniform clothing and accessory items which
contain deficiencies in fit, form, or function, a PQDR (SF 368)
must be submitted per references (t) and (u), via one of the
following methods:

      (1) PQDR submission via the Product Data Reporting and
Evaluation Program (PDREP) located at
http://www.nslcptsmh.navsea.navy.mil/pdrep/pdrep.htm.

      (2) EZ PQDR submission via the USMC PQDR Screening Point
website located at http://www.logcom.usmc.mil/pqdr.

      (3) If web access is not available, PQDRs should be
submitted to the PQDR Screening Point via e-mail attachment to
mailto:mbmatcompqdrs@logcom.usmc.mil.

No repairs to defective items are authorized until
repair/disposition instructions are received from CG,
MARCORLOGCOM in that all clothing and accessory items procured
are covered by various contractual warranties. If the clothing
is urgently needed and the deficiency does not affect the safe
usage of the item or the originator is able to repair the item,
the materiel may be used; however, an advance telephone report
must be made to CG, MARCORLOGCOM (584-2) and the deficiency
information must still be provided via PQDR, providing full
details of the repair, per reference (u).

   c. Quality Deficiency Reports. Upon receipt of non-supply
system, commercial uniform clothing and accessory items that
contain deficiencies in fit, form, or function, a quality
deficiency report (QDR) will be sent directly to:

      CG, MARCORSYSCOM
      Program Manager, Infantry Combat Equipment (PM-ICE)
      2200 Lester Street
      Quantico, VA 22134-6050

2. Checkage Sales. When purchase by cash sales would create a
personal hardship for the customer, a checkage sale is
authorized. Checkage sales will not be used for punitive
purposes, but may be used as a last resort to provide individuals
in a pay status with essential uniform clothing. Because of the

administrative expense and effort required to effect and process a checkage sale, commanders shall ensure compliance with the following specific guidelines:

a. A checkage sale will be authorized only to cover emergency needs of an enlisted person without funds to purchase clothing necessary for health, comfort, or appearance; except when the individual needs clothing incident to confinement per paragraph 2009.4 of this Manual. The requirement to make up shortages for an inspection is not considered an emergency.

b. Checkage sales shall not be authorized if the enlisted person is in a nonpay status, if the dollar value of the sale is less than $50 (except under extraordinary circumstances), or for Marines who are scheduled for separation within 90 days. Validation that the individual is in a pay status must be provided by a copy of the applicable page from the Marine Corps Total Force System unit diary (UD).

c. All checkages must be approved by the commanding officer, and the commanding officer shall hand write the word "certified" in the "approved" block of form NAVMC 604/604B. Only "certified" checkage sales will be honored by issuing activities. Commanding officers shall not "certify" checkages until after arrangements have been made with the disbursing officer in scheduling pay deductions, to alleviate the personal hardship which precluded purchase of the clothing by cash sale.

d. A NAVMC 604/604B will be prepared by the command for all checkage sales. In the event of detachment from the immediate command, the individual's detachment date and destination will be indicated on the front of the form. After approval, the NAVMC 604/604B will be submitted to the MCSS/RCO for issue.

e. The NAVMC 604/604B will be annotated by the MCSS/RCO with only the items issued. The MCSS/RCO will produce three copies of the completed original NAVMC 604/604B and distribute each as follows:

(1) Original to unit or directly to disbursing officer (per local policy and procedures) with completed form SF 1034. It is important that the original be processed quickly through disbursing to ensure the checkage is completed prior to separation by the individual.

(2) Copy to individual.

(3) Copy to unit commander, for placement in the individual's official military personnel file (OMPF).

(4) Copy retained by MCSS/RCO.

3. Special Measurement Orders. Special measurement clothing consists of those items manufactured to the specific measurements of an individual, including orthopedic footwear. Special measurement clothing is authorized for supply only to those individuals who cannot be properly fitted with standard tariff or supplemental sizes or by authorized alterations thereto. The allowance quantity of special measurement clothing shall be the same as that authorized for standard clothing items.

a. Requisitioning Procedures. Requisitions will be submitted per reference (m). The price of special measurement clothing will be the standard price of the item listed in the current standard price list (no mark-up for special measurements). When requisitioning special measurement clothing, the applicable special measurement blank form (DD Form 358 or DD Form 1111) or the Electronic Order Form (EOF) shall be completed and submitted with the requisition.

b. Special Measurements. The measurements to be taken to complete DD Form 358, DD Form 1111, or EOF are self-explanatory.

c. Special Footwear Procedures. Special measurement footwear may be requisitioned for personnel who cannot be fitted from standard tariff size. If it is uncertain as to whether or not a requirement exists for special measurement footwear, the individual will be referred to a Navy medical officer for final determination; the necessity for special measurement footwear (including orthopedic footwear or orthopedic alterations) must be determined by a Navy medical officer. The following additional procedures are required for special footwear:

(1) Medical Authorization. The Navy medical officer must provide a memorandum from the medical facility to the individual's unit containing the following information:

(a) Identification of the individual for whom the footwear is intended.

(b) A signed prescription prepared on a Special Measurement Blank - Boots and Shoes (DD Form 150).

(c) A citation of the local station medical department allotment number and appropriation to be charged for procurement, if the item is considered orthopedic footwear or an orthopedic alteration to standard footwear.

(2) Requisitioning. Upon receipt of the foregoing information, the unit will requisition or request the supporting retail store to requisition the footwear required. When requisitioning for an individual for the first time, a "trial" pair will be ordered. When both low-quarter shoes and boots are required, the trial pair will be boots.

(a) Requisitions for orthopedic or non-commercial special measurement footwear must be submitted through the DSCP C&T website http://www.warfighter.net. A copy of the DD Form 1348 requisition (and accompanying DD Form 150 or comparable form, if required) with a point of contact clearly identified must also be forwarded to the Veterans Administration via fax (212) 951-3247 (Attn: VISN3) or mailed to the Veterans Integrated Service Network 3, Department of Veterans Affairs Medical Center, Attn: Network Prosthetics, 423 East 23rd Street, New York, NY, 10010. Any prescriptions, drawings, tracings, molds, or casts should be forwarded to this Veterans Affairs office.

(b) Requisitions for commercial special measurement footwear (such as goretex lined or poromeric footwear) must be submitted to the DSCP via fax to (215) 737-7429, DSN 444-7429.

(3) Receipt. Upon receipt, the unit will deliver the footwear to the local medical facility for inspection and acceptance; final inspection and acceptance are in all cases the responsibilities of the local medical facility. When footwear does not properly fit the individual, the local medical facility will determine what modifications are required. The local medical facility will appropriately annotate the fitting report and have the footwear and annotated fitting report returned to the Veterans Administration (VISN3) for modification.

(4) Issue or Sale. As stated in paragraph 5004.3.a preceding, special measurement footwear will be sold to authorized individuals at the current standard price. Orthopedic

footwear will be provided as a medical item without charge to the individual. When orthopedic alterations to standard replacement footwear are made, the individual will be required to pay only the standard footwear price.

d. Disposition of Special Measurement Clothing. Excess special measurement clothing may be issued or sold as recovered clothing or turned in to the nearest Defense Reutilization and Marketing Office (DRMO).

4. Not-In-Stock Items. When items required to complete an authorized allowance issue (initial, supplementary, replacement, or miscellaneous) are not-in-stock, the following procedures will be followed:

a. MCRD Initial Issue. See paragraph 3003 preceding.

b. MCSS

(1) Mark "NIS" for "not-in-stock" on the NAVMC 604/604B next to the items which are not available for issue. Provide a copy of the NAVMC 604/604B to the individual.

(2) If the NIS item requires a special order and the individual will be staying at this base/station for sufficient time to receipt for the special order, annotate "SPEC ORDER" next the affected item. Notify the individual or the individual's command upon receipt of the special order items.

c. Unit Commanders. Commanders must ensure that the following procedures are carefully followed, inasmuch as the NAVMC 604/604B constitutes the only authority to make subsequent issues in fulfillment of the individual's authorized allowance.

(1) Upon receipt of the NAVMC 604/604B annotated with NIS items from the individual, prepare a new form NAVMC 604/604B listing those items which were NIS. Annotate the appropriate accounting data applicable at the time of entitlement, as reflected on the NAVMC 604/604B. To ensure that all issues are charged to the correct FY, annotate the individual's current active duty date (CURR ACDU) on the NAVMC 604/604B. The NAVMC 604/604B will be prepared in an original only and will be headed "DUE INDIVIDUAL TO COMPLETE APPLICABLE (list Initial, Supplementary, etc.) ALLOWANCE."

(2) The commanding officer will sign the new NAVMC 604/604B and insert on top of the enlistment contract of the transferring individual's service record book (SRB). The form will be removed upon arrival at the new unit so that remaining items may be issued.

5. Sales to Other Than Regular or Reserve Marines or Sailors. Sales of Marine Corps or Navy uniform clothing is intended primarily for Regular and Reserve Marines and Sailors for their personal use or for the personal use of another authorized patron. Sales to individuals other than Regular or Reserve Marines or Sailors is limited to the following personnel under the specified circumstances, in keeping with the wear regulations of reference (d):

    a. Medal of Honor holders may purchase any Marine Corps uniform.

    b. Retirees may purchase any Marine Corps uniform, as long as the current supply posture ensures availability to active duty personnel. Retirees employed by schools, to include those serving in the Marine Corps Junior Reserve Officer Training Corps (MCJROTC) program, have priority of issue over other retirees. A retired identification card is required for retirees to purchase Marine Corps uniform items.

    c. Former Marines who served honorably during a declared or undeclared war may purchase a Marine Corps service or dress uniform for specified occasions, per reference (w), and the insignia for the highest grade held during such war service. An Armed Forces of the United States Report of Transfer or Discharge (form DD 214-MC) or an Honorable Discharge Certificate (form DD 256) is required as proof of eligible service.

    d. Regular or Reserve Marine Corps or Navy dependents acting as agents for the Marine or Sailor, upon presentation of proper identification (Armed Forces Dependent Identification Card).

    e. Personnel of the U.S. Army or U.S. Air Force may purchase non-Marine Corps distinctive uniform clothing items on an as-available basis when these personnel have not been able to procure the items from their normal source. Marine Corps distinctive items include anything with the Marine Corps emblem, Marine Corps insignia, and Marine Corps unique shirts, trousers, jackets, and covers.

f.   Approved Marine Corps officer candidates.

g.   MCJROTC cadets may purchase individual uniform clothing items as authorized.

h.   DoD contractors, U.S. civilian technicians, and civilian reporters and photographers serving or embedded with the Marine Corps or attending Marine Corps training exercises or operations may purchase or be issued the utility uniform or other mission specific uniform clothing items, when specifically authorized by HQMC.

5005.   ADDITIONAL MILITARY CLOTHING SALES STORE (MCSS) AND SUPPORTED INSTALLATION RESPONSIBILITIES.   In addition to those DC, M&RA responsibilities designated previously in paragraphs 1005, 5003.2, and 5004 of this Manual, installation commanders and DC, M&RA (MR), as the advocate for Marine Corps Community Services (MCCS), have responsibilities, as designated, in the following subcategories:

- Facilities
- Fixtures, Furnishings, and Equipment
- Store Operations
- Clothing Inventory Management
- Record Keeping and Financial Management
- Management Fee

1.   MCSS Facilities

a.   The provision of a suitable and adequate Marine Corps MCSS facility is the responsibility of the installation commanding officer (CO).   Installations are encouraged to locate and operate the MCSS within existing exchange facilities.   Future planning should provide for consolidation within exchange facilities to the maximum extent possible.   Many MCSS operations share sales areas with other MCX resale operations, which are restricted in their use of appropriated funds (APF). Therefore, a careful accounting must be made to determine the portion of business activity that is attributed to the MCSS facility. The method of determining this proportion and for prorating costs will be based on the percentages of the MCSS system uniforms/items adjusted sales (adjusted to reflect a gross margin comparable to the collocated commercial non-system uniform sales) and the commercial non-system uniforms/items to the MCSS facility total sales.

INDIVIDUAL CLOTHING REGULATIONS   5005

    b. Installation COs, in coordination with the installation
Assistant Chief of Staff (AC/S) for MCCS, DC, I&L, and DC, M&RA,
will provide a similar level of commitment to quality of
facilities, equipment and service as provided to other MCCS
facilities on the installation. This commitment is manifest in
the planning, budgeting, and programming of support funds and
improvement projects through the funding sources available under
their respective cognizance. All of the above parties will
coordinate efforts to identify MCSS facility requirements, plan
and develop project documentation, program and budget for the
appropriate construction funding, and seek funding and project
approval from relevant agencies.

    c. Continuing maintenance, repair and support services will
be accomplished through APF sources. Installation AC/S MCCS is
responsible for day-to-day custodial services, minor maintenance
and minor repair of interior surfaces/finishes.

    d. The installation CO and installation AC/S MCCS are
responsible for planning, programming, and budgeting for major
and minor construction, facility maintenance, alterations and
repair, and support services.

    e. The installation commander is responsible for facilities
maintenance, repair, and support services that include, but are
not limited to:

        (1) maintenance and repair to provide structural
integrity

        (2) code and regulatory compliance (e.g., fire and life
safety codes, Occupational Safety and Health Agency (OSHA)
regulations, health and sanitation regulations and environmental
regulations)

        (3) utility systems and heating/air conditioning systems

        (4) all exterior surfaces (including roofing), customer
and staff parking, vehicle circulation systems (e.g., roadways,
traffic lights and service roads), service/delivery areas and
loading docks of facilities operated as MCSS facilities

        (5) utilities payments

        (6) engineering/support services (e.g.,
design/engineering services, fire protection, security, rescue,
pest control, snow removal, sewage, trash and garbage removal,
environmental compliance, sanitation inspections, maintenance of
common grounds, etc.).

f.   Improvements and upgrades to MCSS facilities and the construction of new, expanded and/or replacement Marine Corps MCSS facilities are subject to provisions of references (x) through (z). Examples of improvement and upgrade costs include, but are not limited to:

(1) a prorated share of design and planning costs,

(2) new furnishings and fixtures required to display MCSS merchandise

(3) remodeling and renovation costs associated with the upgrade of the MCSS facility

(4) other costs necessary to keep facilities up to MCCS quality standards

g.   New construction and facility renovation/improvement costs are to be expensed at a prorated amount, per paragraph 5005.1a preceding. The expense amount is calculated by multiplying the total project cost by the appropriate percentage of sales for the MCSS facility.

h.   In-house renovations accomplished by installation forces, may be paid from non-appropriated fund (NAF) sources. If NAF funding is used, improvement expenses are to be depreciated through the management fee, at the prorated amount, per paragraph 5005.6 following.

2.   Fixtures, Furnishings, and Equipment

a.   Fixtures, furnishings, and equipment required as part of the initial outfitting of new construction and expansion projects will be procured by MCCS, and will be depreciated through the management fee, per paragraph 5005.6 following. The cost of equipment replacement will be prorated as provided in paragraph 5005.1a, preceding.

b.   Installation MCCS representatives will have maintenance and custodial responsibility of the MCSS store fixtures and furnishings. When determined unserviceable by MCCS, fixtures, furnishings and equipment used in the sale of MCSS merchandise will be replaced by MCCS with NAF funding. The cost of equipment replacement will be prorated per paragraph 5005.1a preceding. The resulting cost of the replacement Marine Corps MCSS equipment will be reimbursed by depreciation through the management fee, per paragraph 5005.6 following.

3.   Store Operations

a.   Commercially procured non-system articles of uniform clothing must contain certification of approval from CG,

MARCORSYSCOM (PM-ICE), per reference (d). When commercially procured uniform clothing items are displayed, the corresponding system item shall be displayed with similar visibility.

b. Recovered clothing shall be sold and displayed separate from new items and appropriately identified.

c. MCSS facilities are authorized to stock and sell Navy system and commercial uniforms/items.

d. Quality control procedures will be conducted per reference (u) for system items and per reference (d) for non-system commercial/optional uniform items.

e. Operating hours of Marine Corps MCSS facilities will be established by the local command.

4. Clothing Inventory Management

a. MCCS personnel will purchase, control, store, and distribute MCSS clothing inventories. This responsibility does not include war reserve stock management. Purchasing and stocking requirements are as follows:

(1) Purchase established sizes of clothing, footwear, and special measurement clothing from approved sources (most often DSCP). Special measurement footwear will be purchased from the Defense Orthopedic Footwear Clinic, Boston, MA.

(2) Purchase those items that, because of a low demand do not warrant stockage, from the approved source of supply on a special order basis.

(3) Stock and ensure reasonable availability, for sale and issue, those clothing items that have been prescribed for wear by CMC and designated in reference (c).

(4) Stock, for sale only, a selection of merchandise designated as organizational ICCE (782 gear, etc.). Items selected will include those authorized in reference (d), as well as items prone to being lost, damaged, or destroyed, and for which the individual Marine is accountable. Only limited quantities of selected ICCE items will be stocked.

b. MCCS will transfer military clothing items obtained from DSCP to non-MCCS activities as directed by DC, I&L. Transportation expenses incurred by MCCS if any, for such transfers, are considered operating expenses of the Marine Corps MCSS and are reimbursable through the management fee, per paragraph 5005.6 following.

c. Assist DC, I&L and CG, MARCORSYSCOM (PM-ICE) in phasing out all clothing items being replaced or deleted from the military clothing system.

5. Record Keeping and Financial Management

a. Perform fiscal accounting, per chapter 3 of this Manual.

b. Installation MCSS activities will also maintain record of sales consisting of:

(1) Control of cash registers and reporting of transactions in accordance with DC, M&RA (MR) policies and procedures

(2) A minimum of two different cash register keys must be used to record merchandise purchased from commercial vendors, merchandise purchased from supply system suppliers or recovered clothing, and authorized alterations and exchanges (i.e. these types of sales shall not be commingled). Alterations will be managed per paragraph 2009.2 of this Manual. MCSS merchandise purchased from DSCP may be exchanged per MCSS policy.

c. The original MCSS inventory was created by a NWCF loan. MARCORLOGCOM increases the money value of the initial loan, as required, so that the MCSSs can maintain sufficient stock to support each installation's requirements. MARCORLOGCOM provides additional NWCF resources as follows:

(1) Inventory of DSCP merchandise on hand.

(2) DSCP merchandise in transit (i.e., paid for by MCSS but not yet received).

(3) In transit losses that are not offset by in transit gains or credits for reporting of supply discrepancies, per reference (aa).

(4) DSCP merchandise sold/issued through forms NAVMC 604/604B and not yet reimbursed.

(5) Annual price change or write-offs of DSCP merchandise.

d. Annual price change or write-offs of DSCP merchandise. Price changes of DSCP merchandise are categorized as follows:

(1) DSCP Discounts/Markdowns. Price reductions to promote the sale of phase out DSCP items as directed by CG, MARCORLOGCOM.

        (2) Salable Recovered Clothing. Price reductions for
salable DSCP items in other than condition code "A," as
determined by the MCSS.

        (3) Price increases directed by DSCP.

        (4) DSCP write-offs for disposal; markdowns to "zero" for
non—salable or defective items turned into DRMO.

        (5)As directed in writing by DC, I&L.

     e. The adequacy of NWCF for the preceding assets and
activities will be periodically determined by DC, M&RA (MR) and
verified by CG, MARCORLOGCOM. Adjustment of funds either by
withdrawing excess funds or providing additional NWCF resources
will then be made as mutually agreed upon by DC, M&RA and CG,
MARCORLOGCOM.

6. Management Fee. MCSS cost centers are break-even operations.
This is accomplished through an MCSS Management Fee to reimburse
the costs associated with MCSS operations. The MCSS Management
Fees will be computed concurrently with the closing of the
previous month's MCX operations, in accordance with the guidance
contained in MCCS financial management policies. The computed
management fees and documentation will be submitted to M&RA (MRF)
for review and subsequent reimbursement through the
installations' MCCS Concentration Bank account.

INDIVIDUAL CLOTHING REGULATIONS

CHAPTER 6

CLOTHING RETENTION, RECOVERY, AND REPLACEMENT

INDIVIDUAL CLOTHING REGULATIONS

CHAPTER 6

CLOTHING RETENTION, RECOVERY, AND REPLACEMENT

6000. INTRODUCTION. This chapter provides policy and procedures involving the retention, recovery, and replacement of issued uniform clothing and disposition of recovered clothing.

6001. SCOPE. This policy and these procedures pertain to personnel of the Regular and Reserve establishment (unless otherwise specified).

6002. CLOTHING RETENTION. Except as provided in paragraph 6003 following, enlisted personnel upon separation may retain all articles of individual uniform clothing that were issued for retention during their service. Prior to effecting the separation of an individual, either from active to reserve duty or from obligated service, commanders shall ensure that a clothing exit inventory is conducted and recorded on form NAVMC 631/631A (see paragraph 3004 preceding) which will become a permanent part of the individual's official military personnel file (OMPF). Commanders shall also ensure that enlisted Marines who are separated understand that uniform clothing will be retained as follows:

1. "Obligors" (Still Under Contract for Obligated Individual Ready Reserve (IRR), Individual Mobilization Augmentee (IMA), or Selected Marine Corps Reserve (SMCR) Service). While in an obligor status, individuals must maintain the MRL of uniform clothing at the time of their release from active duty.

   a. If obligors are recalled to active duty or directed to report for further service with any Marine Corps Reserve organization or if they reenlist, they will be required to bring with them all individual uniform clothing items which were possessed at the time of release from active duty.

   b. If activated obligors do not return with all the required uniform clothing, commanders will conduct an investigation to determine whether there is fault or negligence on the part of the individual for not reporting with all the required clothing.

c. If fault or negligence is determined, only clothing which
was either recovered or not issued during the previous enlistment
may be issued at no expense to the individual. In such cases,
deficiencies will be replaced by the individual via cash sales or
checkage.

2. "Non-Obligors" (No Longer Under Contract and Released or
Retired From Obligated Service). Individuals that are
discharged, retired, or otherwise released from a contract to
obligated service must maintain the Minimum Requirements List
(MRL) of uniform clothing at the time of their release from
obligated service for a minimum of 3 months.

    a. If non-obligors are recalled to active duty or directed
to report for further service with any Marine Corps Reserve
organization or if they reenlist within 3 months after completion
of Marine Corps obligated service, they will be required to bring
with them all individual uniform clothing items which were
possessed upon last discharge from active duty.

    b. If activated non-obligors do not return with all the
required uniform clothing, commanders will conduct an
investigation to determine whether there is fault or negligence
on the part of the individual for not reporting with all the
required clothing.

    c. If fault or negligence is determined, only clothing which
was either recovered or not issued during the previous enlistment
may be issued at no expense to the individual. In such cases,
deficiencies will be replaced by the individual via cash sales or
checkage.

    d. Recalled non-obligors who activate, are directed to
reserve duty, or reenlist in the Marine Corps at a time which is
beyond the third month following their discharge from all
obligated service, shall be entitled to a complete Initial Issue,
per paragraph 2003 of this Manual.

3. Officer Candidates. Officer candidates will be required to
retain individual uniform clothing for use until successful
completion of OCS, unless separated from the program for a cause
other than appointment. The individual will be permitted to
retain, for military use, all uniform clothing furnished under
the provisions of these regulations.

4. <u>Conscientious Objectors</u>. Personnel who are honorably discharged by reason of declaration as a conscientious objector may retain all clothing in their possession.

6003. <u>CLOTHING RECOVERY</u>. Issued uniform clothing will be recovered, as detailed below, from the following personnel:

- Personnel Discharged Under Exceptional Circumstances
- Personnel Who Have Served 6 Months or Less on Active Duty
- Enlisted Personnel Discharged to Accept a Direct Commission of Appointment as a Marine Officer
- Prisoners
- Personnel in an Unauthorized Absence (UA) or Deserter Status
- Navy Personnel Failing to Complete Field Medical School (FMS)
- Officer Candidates

1. <u>Recovery from Personnel Discharged Under Exceptional Circumstances</u>. All articles of uniform clothing, less worn socks, underclothing, general purpose trunks, gloves, and footwear, either initially issued or purchased via a paid cash clothing allowance, must be recovered from individuals discharged for the following reasons:

- Defective enlistment and inductions
- Entry level performance and conduct
- Unsatisfactory performance
- Homosexual conduct
- Drug abuse rehabilitation failure
- Alcohol abuse rehabilitation failure
- Misconduct
- Separation in lieu of trial by court martial
- Interned or discharged as alien enemies
- Positive results on entrance drug and alcohol test
- Security (i.e., security violations, breaches, etc.)

Individuals discharged for the reasons set forth above must have adequate clothing for wear to their home. If the individuals do not have sufficient clothes for traveling, the activity commander may authorize the issue of a Minimum Traveling Uniform, less insignia, per paragraph 2009 of this Manual.

2. <u>Recovery from Personnel Who Have Served 6 Months or Less on Active Duty</u>. Individuals who have served 6 months or less on active duty, subsequent to the last authorization to an initial clothing allowance or supplementary clothing allowance issue, will be permitted to retain only worn socks, underclothing, general purpose trunks, gloves, footwear, and one complete seasonal uniform for travel.

3. <u>Recovery from Enlisted Personnel Discharged to Accept a Direct Commission of Appointment as a Marine Officer</u>. Enlisted personnel discharged to accept a direct commission or appointment as a Marine officer may retain all clothing in their possession.

4. <u>Recovery from Prisoners</u>. Individual uniform clothing, less worn socks, underclothing, general purpose trunks, gloves, and footwear and items required incident to confinement, will be recovered from prisoners, upon approval of a sentence involving confinement and punitive discharge, and maintained until the individual is released from confinement.

5. <u>Recovery from Personnel in an Unauthorized Absence (UA) or Deserter Status</u>. Individual uniform clothing for personnel in a UA or Deserter status will be recovered and inventoried per reference (s).

6. <u>Recovery from Navy Personnel Failing to Complete Field Medical School (FMS)</u>. Individual uniform clothing issued, less worn socks, underclothing, general purpose trunks, and gloves will be collected from Navy personnel who fail to successfully complete FMS, for reasons other than medical.

7. <u>Recovery from Officer Candidates</u>. When an officer candidate is separated from an officer procurement program for cause other than appointment, the disposition of clothing in the individual's possession will be governed by the individual's Marine Corps affiliation after separation from the program. In all cases, clothing issued to the individual will be inventoried and verified. Upon recovery of the clothing, a signed receipt will be provided to the individual. If fault or negligence on behalf

of the individual for loss or damage is determined by the
activity commander, the individual will be required to bear the
replacement cost of such clothing.

a. When an individual will continue to serve on active duty
in an enlisted status with the Marine Corps, clothing items
issued which are in excess to the applicable MRL for personnel of
the Regular Establishment shall be recovered. However, all worn
socks, underclothing, general purpose trunks, headgear, and
gloves may be retained by the individual for further use.
Enlisted personnel that have previously received an initial
clothing allowance and will be returning to an enlisted status
with the Regular establishment will be issued the remaining
clothing required to bring their issue up to the current active
duty MRL.

b. For those enlisted personnel who were issued a new
complete Initial Issue for the officer procurement program but do
not successfully complete the program and are disenrolled, the
date of disenrollment will be considered as the date of
entitlement to that initial clothing allowance. Six months from
the date of disenrollment, the individual will become entitled to
the accrual of BCRA.

c. When an individual will continue to serve in the Marine
Corps Reserve, all clothing items on charge to the individual,
less worn underclothing, boots, socks, general purpose trunks,
and headgear which are in excess to the applicable Reserve MRL,
shall be recovered.

d. All clothing issued, less worn underclothing and socks,
to unsuccessful and completely discharged candidates shall be
recovered.

6004. DISPOSITION OF RECOVERED CLOTHING. Instructions for the
collecting, inventorying, storing, and disposing of abandoned or
unclaimed uniform clothing or uniform clothing of personnel who
come into any status whereby they cannot or do not care for their
own property are contained in reference (s). This includes
uniform clothing for those who die, are reported missing, are
incapacitated by injury or disease, are in an unauthorized
absence/deserter status, and those who for any other reason
become separated from their effects. In addition, chapter 9 of

this Manual contains instructions regarding the handling of
uniform clothing for personnel transferred to and from combat
areas.

1. Disposition of Unserviceable Recovered Clothing.
Unserviceable items will be disposed of via the closest Defense
Reutilization and Marketing Office (DRMO) per current disposal
instructions.

2. Disposition of Serviceable Condition Code A or B Recovered
Clothing. Serviceable new, used, repaired, or reconditioned
recovered uniform clothing with more than 6 months of useful
service life (condition code A, per reference (bb)) or with 3 to
6 months of useful service life for applicable issues (condition
code B, per reference (bb)) will be made available for issue or
sale. Condition code A and B clothing includes worn clothing
which has been marked internally by the previous owner, but can
be remarked per reference (d). Condition code A or B recovered
clothing will be processed as follows:

    a. Commands supported by a local Military Clothing Sales
Store (MCSS)/Retail Clothing Outlet (RCO) will turn in excess
condition code A or B clothing to that MCSS/RCO. The MCSS/RCO
will first attempt to sell or issue recovered clothing; condition
code A items at the current FY unit price and condition code B
items at a price based on the market and the condition of the
items. This policy for condition code B items allows the store
flexibility in setting the sales price, which in turn assists in
selling a greater quantity of recovered clothing, provides
Marines with a more economical source of uniforms, and reduces
the quantity of serviceable uniform items transferred to
disposal.

    b. Commands not supported by a local MCSS/RCO may retain an
amount up to a projected 180-day requirement of condition code A
or B recovered clothing. This requirement is to be based on the
issues/sales for the previous 180 days. Additional excesses may
be shipped to the nearest MCSS/RCO (upon coordination) or should
be handled per paragraph c following.

    c. Every attempt should be made to reutilize excess
condition code A or B clothing through redistribution. Excess
serviceable clothing may be shipped to the nearest Marine Corps
Recruit Depot (MCRD), upon coordination, using a transfer

document (DD Form 1348-1) as outlined in UM 4400-15. Transportation costs will be negotiated between both parties. Additional excesses should be reported to MARCORLOGCOM, Supply Chain Management, Materiel Distribution and Management Department (584-2) for potential redistribution or disposed of via the closest DRMO per current disposal instructions. During initial fielding of new clothing items, when demand is high, but stocks are low, disposition of excess clothing items must be approved by MARCORLOGCOM (584-2).

d. MCRDs may make recovered uniform clothing available to the Marine Corps Districts for distribution to Marine Corps Junior Reserve Officer Training Corps (MCJROTC) units. MCJROTC units should provide requirements for recovered uniform clothing to their district supply offices. In turn, District supply offices should submit requirements to the closest MCRD (Parris Island, SC for JROTC units east of the Mississippi and San Diego, CA for JROTC units west of the Mississippi). Recovered uniform clothing may be shipped directly from the MCRDs to MCJROTC units, if the service does not interfere with primary mission accomplishment and if sufficient manpower resources are available. However, the MCRDs will not serve as a "mail order service" for the MCJROTC units.

6005. CLOTHING REPLACEMENT. References (a) and (b) direct that service members shall be compensated for clothing items destroyed, damaged, lost, abandoned, captured, or otherwise rendered unusable, incident to military training or service, if the loss was not caused by any fault or negligence of the member. The Marine Corps fulfills this requirement via replacement issues, using forms NAVMC 604/604B as proper documentation. Clothing items furnished as replacement issues may be either new or serviceable recovered clothing suitable for resale. Routine replacement of enlisted issued uniform clothing for normal wear and tear is to be performed by individuals using their CRA, per paragraph 2006 preceding. Replacement of authorized civilian clothing allowances is provided per paragraph 2007.1a(2) of this Manual. The clothing replacements detailed below are for clothing items destroyed, damaged, lost, abandoned, captured, or otherwise rendered unusable beyond normal wear and tear and through no fault of negligence by the individual.

1. <u>Clothing Replacement Issues Categories</u>. Replacement issues
fall into one of the following categories:

    a. <u>Miscellaneous Issues/Replacements Issues</u>. This category
of replacement issues includes a variety of miscellaneous
replacements to returned prisoners of war, authorized personnel
for burial of the dead, personnel authorized by the Personal
Property Claims Regulations of the JAG Manual (see paragraph
2009.7 preceding), absentees and deserters restored to full time
duty, prisoners requiring a Minimum Traveling Uniform, and other
issues described in paragraph 2009.4-8 and in Figure 3-1 of this
Manual. Functional Account Number (FAN) "72048" is used for
these replacements.

    b. <u>Replacement Issues Incident to Military Training or
Service in a Combat Area</u>. See paragraph 9004.2 following.

    c. <u>Replacement Issues Incident to Military Training or
Service Outside of Combat</u>. Personnel assigned to duties that may
prematurely damage or destroy uniform clothing items should be
issued coveralls or other garments. If adequate protective
garments were not available, uniform items must be replaced at
unit expense (local Operations and Maintenance, Marine Corps
(O&MMC) expense), as a personal property claim is not applicable.
Specific instances when this replacement is authorized include
when uniforms are lost or rendered unserviceable due to military
conveyance, contamination, individual physical profile changes
due to medical condition (significant weight loss or gain due to
illness or other medical condition), emergency first aid, and
military operated laundry. These replacement issues will be
locally funded using unit O&MMC funds; unit appropriation data
must be provided on the NAVMC 604/604B. When clothing is
prematurely damaged, destroyed, or lost aboard a Navy vessel,
replacement should first be requested via the officer-in-charge
of the Marine Corps Detachment to the ship's supply officer.

    d. <u>Replacement Issues or Minimum Combat Load Issues to
Mobilized Enlisted Reservists and other Activated Personnel on
Extended Active Duty</u>. See paragraph 9002.1 following.

    e. <u>Special Blue Uniform Replacement Allowance Issues</u>. See
paragraph 2008.3.c preceding.

f. Replacement Issues During Recruit Training. Clothing furnished as part of the Initial Issue will be replaced at anytime during training if the item is found to be defective due to a manfacturers defect. Exchanges for improper fit will be permitted for a limited duration of the training schedule (i.e., within the first 25 days), as designated by the local commander. Recruits must exchange the same sized item that they were issued. Recruits should not be permitted to leave the depot without a complete Initial Issue, unless proper documentation is provided indicating that a particular item was not available, per paragraph 3003 of this Manual.

g. Replacement Issues During Officer Candidate School (OCS). Clothing furnished during OCS will be replaced at Government expense when it has been determined that clothing on charge to candidates has been unavoidably lost, damaged, or worn out to a degree warranting replacement. However, applicable enlisted candidates will be required to purchase replacement clothing using their CRA. Clothing furnished will be replaced at the candidate's expense when the activity commander determines that the candidate was at fault or negligent for items lost, damaged, or worn to a degree warranting replacement.

h. Replacements for Defective Items Issued or Purchased. Replacements for uniform clothing items found to be defective due to manufacturer defects should be replaced by the issuing organization, when an original receipt or other proof of purchase/issue is provided and the item is still in its purchased condition. The issuing facility will initiate a PQDR per paragraph 5004 of this Manual. Suspected manufacturer defects on worn or used clothing will be investigated and handled on a case-by-case basis.

i. Replacements In-Kind for Enlisted Selected Marine Corps Reservists. See paragraph 8002 following.

2. Policy and Procedures for Replacement Issues.

a. Replacement issues must be completed on a one-for-one basis, with unserviceable items being recovered, whenever possible, in order to prevent waste, fraud, or abuse. All replacements should be done only on a case-by-case basis; unit wide replacement issues are prohibited, except that replacement

of organizational clothing issued for sustainment during combat
is permitted on a unit-wide basis, per paragraph 9005 of this
Manual.

    b.   Replacement issues in categories a-c and h in paragraph
6005.1 preceding are authorized to both officers and enlisted
Marines and Navy personnel serving with Marine Corps units
(Marine uniform system clothing items only). Claims for
additional items may be requested via a personal property claim,
per paragraph 2009.7 of this Manual. All other claims are
applicable to enlisted personnel only.

    c.   Approval. Category a and b replacement issues described
in paragraph 6005.1 preceding must be approved by the Major
Subordinate Commander (MSC) or higher (i.e., HQMC). All other
replacement issues must be approved by the unit commander.

    d.   Documentation. All replacement issues must be documented
on forms NAVMC 604/604B. Applicable information from the NAVMC
604/604B will be transferred to the NAVMC 631/631B and filed in
the individual's OMPF, per paragraph 3004 of this Manual.

INDIVIDUAL CLOTHING REGULATIONS

CHAPTER 7

ORGANIZATIONAL CLOTHING AND EQUIPMENT

CHAPTER 7

ORGANIZATIONAL CLOTHING AND EQUIPMENT

7000. <u>INTRODUCTION</u>. Organizational clothing and equipment are significantly different from other uniform clothing discussed in this Manual, in that organizational clothing and equipment remains the property of the U.S. Government, unless otherwise designated in writing by HQMC.

7001. <u>SCOPE</u>. The organizational clothing and equipment discussed in this chapter is issued by a using unit or authorized consolidated issue facility/organization based on the mission the individual will be performing. Strict adherence to the following organizational issue policy is required to avoid waste, fraud, and/or abuse.

7002. <u>DEFINITION</u>

1. Organizational clothing and equipment are those items on a unit/organization's allowance list designed for temporary issue to individuals; including table of equipment (T/E) or other items approved in writing by Headquarters Marine Corps (HQMC) through the Universal Need Statement (UNS) or other designated process. Organizational clothing is that clothing which is either provided through initial fielding or purchased using Operations and Maintenance, Marine Corps (O&MMC) funds vice MILPERS appropriations. The individual is accountable for organizational clothing and equipment issued and all organizationally issued clothing and equipment will be recovered prior to the reassignment of the individual to other duties, except for items designed for personal retention specified in paragraph 7003.2 following. Organizational clothing and equipment will be issued only at the discretion of the commander, according to guidelines and directives published by HQMC.

2. To establish a new allowance for organizational clothing (i.e. for which a T/E does not already exist), organizations must submit an UNS via the Combat Development Tracking System (CDTS) website at <u>https://www.cdts.marcorsyscom.usmc.mil</u>.

7003. TYPES OF ORGANIZATIONAL CLOTHING AND EQUIPMENT

1. Uniform Clothing. Uniform clothing items issued as part of the Initial Issue (aka seabag) to individuals for permanent retention may also be issued organizationally, if required for special missions. This includes sustainment issues during combat operations. However, special handling and controls are required to prevent waste, fraud, and abuse, per paragraph 7005 following.

2. Personal Retention Items. Personal retention items are those select items designed for permanent issue or clothing items that are worn close to the body, so that it would be unhygienic to recover them following use by an individual. Personal retention items include:

    a. Trunk lockers, suitcases, wetsuits, swimmers' shoes, and safety shoes. Per reference (cc), these items will be issued for retention, as available, to commissioned officers, warrant officers, and SNCOs. Documentation will be made for Staff Noncommissioned Officers (SNCOs) per paragraph 3004 of this Manual and via appropriate entry per reference (h).

    b. Head gear, underwear, t-shirts, socks, and footwear, which are worn close to the body. Per references (h) and (n), some of these items will be recovered (specific quantities of campaign hats, etc.).

3. Class II Individual Combat Clothing and Equipment (ICCE) (782 gear). Regular Class II ICCE is typically issued to individuals for the duration of their tour at a particular duty station. Class II ICCE includes 782 gear such as helmets, outer tactical vests, individual first aid kits, and cold weather jackets. Class II ICCE is maintained primarily in Consolidated Issue Facilities (CIFs) at each major base/station. Units not supported by a CIF continue to maintain Class II ICCE at the unit level.

4. TAM Type 3 Contingency ICCE. TAM Type 3 Contingency ICCE is that special equipment maintained for unique contingency or training evolutions. Type 3 ICCE requires special measures of control since it is used for particular conditions or situations, such as for cold weather or desert operations. Type 3 ICCE includes coveralls, cold weather clothing, desert clothing,

aviation clothing and other special equipment. Type 3 ICCE
allowances are established by the operating forces and loaded to
equipment allowance files. Type 3 ICCE is not normally
maintained at the using unit level, except during deployments.
When not issued out to using units or individuals, Type 3 ICCE is
maintained in a special allowance pool (e.g., Contingency
Training Equipment Pool (CTEP), Training Allowance Pool (TAP), or
another authorized consolidated facility).

5. Nuclear, Biological, and Chemical Defense Equipment (NBCDE).
NBCDE includes NBC personal protective equipment or clothing that
is worn when and as prescribed by the commander. NBCDE is
maintained at either the using unit level or at an authorized
consolidated storage and issue facility.

7004. MARKING OF ORGANIZATIONAL CLOTHING AND EQUIPMENT.
Organizational clothing and equipment will be adequately marked
to provide positive identification separate from gratuitous
issues to individuals or personally purchased clothing.
Organizational commanders have the flexibility to temporarily
mark equipment, as they deem appropriate or necessary, within the
following guidelines:

1. No article will be altered for an individual to the extent
that it cannot be re-altered for issue to another individual.

2. Marking is permitted, as long as the marking is not permanent
(except by personnel specifically authorized per paragraph 7004.3
following) and does not damage or degrade the combat
effectiveness of the items.

3. Use of permanent ink is specifically prohibited except for by
authorized CIF/CTEP or other HQMC directed consolidated issue
facility/organization. In these exceptional cases, permanent
marking by authorized personnel that does not damage or degrade
the combat effectiveness of the clothing and equipment is
authorized to identify it as Government owned property and to
segregate it from individually issued or personally owned
clothing and equipment. Those personal retention items described
in paragraph 7003.2 preceding may be marked in any way deemed
appropriate by the individual at his/her own cost.

4. Organizational clothing and equipment that is drawn from a CIF, CTEP/TAP, or other authorized consolidated issue facility/organization should be marked only in accordance with the facility/organization's Standard Operating Procedures (SOP).

5. Special care should be taken by individuals when drawing organizational clothing and equipment. Individuals should be instructed to closely inspect the clothing or equipment upon issue to ensure there are no permanent markings for which they might be held responsible upon turn-in.

6. The sewing on of removable labels, to include name and service tapes, to organizational clothing and equipment is permitted at the discretion of the organizational commander as long as this procedure does not damage the clothing or equipment or degrade its combat effectiveness. Name and service tapes may be sewn on to the extended cold weather clothing system (ECWCS aka Goretex) in a manner that does not damage the weather-proof integrity of the item, specifically as follows:

    a. Name tapes can be sewn on to the right shoulder pocket flap and service tapes to the left shoulder pocket flap of the parka.

    b. Name tapes can be sewn on to the right seat pocket flap of the trousers.

7. The cost of name and service tapes and the cost of the service to sew them on to organizational clothing and equipment must be provided at Government expense using local O&MMC funds. Individuals cannot be directed to pay for the name or service tapes or the service of sewing them on.

8. Special care should be taken by individuals when removing name tapes so as to prevent damage. Service tapes should be left on organizational clothing and equipment.

9. Ironing on of the Marine Corps emblem (eagle, globe, and anchor) to helmet covers is authorized

10. Other means, to include using baggage tags or twist tie labels, should be considered to temporarily mark organizational clothing and equipment with no risk of damage.

7005. ACCOUNTING FOR ORGANIZATIONAL CLOTHING AND EQUIPMENT

1. Allowances. Commanders may issue whatever organizational clothing or equipment is necessary for mission accomplishment, as long as local allowances are established. Whenever possible, allowances should be consolidated and items maintained at a central facility such as the CIF, CTEP/TAP, or other authorized consolidated issue facility/organization.

2. Funding. Only local O&MMC appropriations may be used to purchase organizational clothing and equipment.

3. Requisitioning. To the maximum extent possible, orders for organizational clothing and equipment should be conducted by the supporting CIF, CTEP/TAP, or other authorized consolidated issue facility/organization. Initial requirements for all deploying personnel should be planned and ordered for issue prior to deployment. During deployment, requisitions for sustainment organizational clothing and equipment should be managed by the supporting Combat Logistics Element (CLE). At locations where no authorized consolidated issue facility/organization is available, individual requisitions for authorized personnel may be processed through a supporting supply organization or an MCSS/RCO. Any authorized method that provides local O&MMC appropriation data for the purchase may be used, including forms NAVMC 604/604B.

4. Recovery. Organizationally issued clothing and equipment will be accounted for as nonexpendable property and must be recovered prior to the reassignment of the individual to other duties, except for items specifically designed for personal retention and specified in paragraph 7003.2 preceding. Any organizationally issued clothing and equipment that is not recovered must be completely and properly vouchered, per reference (cc). Recovered clothing will be processed for reissue or disposed of in the best interest of the U.S. Government, if the condition so warrants.

5. Laundering. Laundry services for organizational clothing and equipment will be paid for using unit O&MMC funding and cannot be charged to individuals.

INDIVIDUAL CLOTHING REGULATIONS

CHAPTER 8

RESERVE CLOTHING

CHAPTER 8

RESERVE CLOTHING

8000. <u>INTRODUCTION</u>. This chapter provides policy and procedures for additional clothing administration by the Marine Corps Reserve establishment.

8001. <u>SCOPE</u>. This policy and these procedures pertain only to personnel of the Reserve establishment. Commander, Marine Corps Forces Reserve (COMMARFORRES) will supplement this policy, as necessary, with Reserve directives. Additional Reserve clothing administration policy and procedures are provided in earlier chapters, where not specific only to the Reserve establishment.

8002. <u>DEFINITION</u>. Enlisted Reserve clothing is issued under the <u>replacement in-kind process</u>, whereby items of uniform clothing are initially furnished as required and replacement thereafter is accomplished by a direct exchange of garments (serviceable for unserviceable). With the replacement in-kind process, no Clothing Replacement Allowance (CRA) is provided. Replacements are made on an item-for-item basis and individual clothing records are maintained to document the amounts of clothing issued and on charge to an individual.

8003. <u>ENTITLEMENT</u>

1. Clothing allowances for enlisted reserve personnel, including initial clothing allowances, are specified in chapter 2 preceding and annually in reference (c). Those contained in the current reserve Minimum Requirements List (MRL) are authorized for replacement in-kind to enlisted personnel of the Marine Corps Reserve under the conditions prescribed for each allowance and subject to the restrictions contained in paragraph 8004 following.

2. Reserve enlisted personnel assigned to active duty for training in excess of 30 days will possess, at a minimum, those items contained in the Reserve MRL.

3. Enlisted Reserve personnel in an Individual Ready Reserve (IRR) or Individual Moblization Augmentee (IMA) status may be issued, under the replacement in-kind system, only clothing which was either recovered or not previously issued by Regular Marine Corps or Selected Marine Corps Reserve (SMCR) units up to the Reserve MRL. Replacement in-kind may only be done upon specific approval of the CG, Mobilization Command (MOBCOM) or when activated, per chapter 9 of this Manual.

4. Personnel enlisting in the Marine Corps Reserve after being separated from a service other than the Marine Corps will be provided clothing via the replacement in-kind process. Entitlement to the applicable allowance(s) is authorized without regard to clothing retained upon separation from the other service.

8004. RESTRICTIONS TO ENTITLEMENT. Enlisted personnel of the Marine Corps or Navy (assigned to Marine Corps units), who have previously been issued clothing as an Initial Clothing Allowance or Supplementary Clothing Allowance while on active duty in the Marine Corps, will use such clothing in performing Reserve service. Individuals reporting for further service with a Marine Corps Reserve organization after being separated from active duty shall be required to report with all individual uniform clothing items in their possession.

1. Clothing deficient to that contained in the Reserve MRL may be provided via the replacement in-kind process when it has been determined by the unit commander that no fault or negligence on the part of the individual is involved.

2. Clothing deficient to that contained in the Reserve MRL will be replaced by the individual, by cash sales or checkage, when it is determined by the unit commander that there is fault or negligence on the part of the individual.

8005. ISSUE AND SALES PROCEDURES. Either new or serviceable recovered clothing suitable for resale may be furnished personnel via the replacement in-kind process or cash sale/checkage.

1. Clothing Requests. Enlisted personnel requiring clothing will use a Combined Individual Clothing Requisition and Issue Slip (form NAVMC 604/604B) to request such clothing. These forms

may be downloaded from the Marine Corps Electronic Forms System (MCEFS) located at http://www.hqmc.usmc.mil/ar/recmgmt.nsf. NAVMC 604/604B will be prepared per the instructions outlined herein.

    a. A separate NAVMC 604/604B is required for:

        (1) Issues, in duplicate.

        (2) Cash sales, in duplicate.

        (3) Checkage sales, in triplicate.

    b. A properly prepared NAVMC 604/604B will be submitted by the individual to the unit commander for approval and forwarding to the unit responsible officer. Preparation instructions are contained on page two of this form.

2. Approval. The unit commander (or other officer assigned in writing to sign "by-direction" for the commander) must approve and certify the NAVMC 604/604B, as this form involves the direct expenditure of Government funds. Certification is done through clothing inspections and reconciliation with the Individual Clothing Record (NAVMC 631/631A) and prescribed allowances. The approved NAMVC 604/604B will be forwarded to the responsible officer for appropriate action. In approving sales, unit commanders shall ensure that all articles sold are for the specific use of the individual concerned. Individual clothing issued or sold to these personnel is intended for wear while performing Reserve duty; it is not intended for wear for civilian work purposes or other unofficial wear by the individual. Checkage sales may be approved per paragraph 5004.2 of this Manual.

3. Requisitioning. Upon receipt of an approved NAVMC 604/604B, requirements for like items will be consolidated for requisition by the ordering unit.

    a. The name(s) of the individual(s) will be annotated in the "remarks" section of the unit supply document register, in order to relate document numbers to the supporting NAVMC 604/604B.

    b. Pending receipt of clothing, NAVMC 604/604B forms will be
filed in alphabetical sequence.

    c. Reserve units will requisition all clothing items from
the KY Logistics Operation Center (KYLOC) website www.KYLOC.com.
KYLOC is the sole source for Reserve clothing acquisitions.

    d. Requisitioning instructions for replacement issues of the
women's black pump dress shoes are contained in reference (bb).

    e. The total cost of uniform clothing issued to SMCR
personnel will be charged to the Reserve Military Personnel,
Marine Corps (MILPERS) appropriation current at the time the
issue actually occurs.

4. Issues

    a. Segregate the clothing received, utilizing the retained
copy of the requisition for determining items requested by the
individual.

    b. Initial/Replacement Issues. The reservist will initial
the NAVMC 604/604B after the items are received. Upon completion
of the issue, the reservist will sign the NAVMC 604/604B in the
space provided. The original form supports the disposition of
the clothing received. It must be annotated with the correct
fund code and other financial data, per figure 3-1 of this Manual
and filed in alphabetical sequence by Fiscal Year (FY). Copies
will be distributed as follows:

        (1) Initial Issues. Utilized for completion of the NAVMC
631/631A and then destroyed.

        (2) Replacement Issues. Filed directly behind the NAVMC
631/631A, held in the unit supply section.

5. Cash Sales and Checkages. The cash or checkage sale of all
items of individual uniform clothing to personnel of the Marine
Corps Reserve is authorized. These sales will be accomplished as
follows:

    a. Replacement issues for articles of clothing avoidably
lost or destroyed shall be accomplished by cash sale or checkage
of the individual's pay account.

b. Per paragraph 5004 of this Manual, checkage sales are not authorized unless a personal hardship would accrue.

c. An approved NAVMC 604/604B shall be used as the sales slip when cash or checkage sales of individual uniform clothing are made from Marine Corps Reserve unit stocks.

d. Upon completion of a Reserve unit cash or checkage sale, the reservist will sign the NAVMC 604/604B in the space provided to indicate receipt of authorized items. The selling unit will annotate the NAVMC 604/604B to indicate receipt of payment (if a cash sale) or completion of the sale via checkage.

(1) For cash sales, the original initialed, signed, and receipted NAVMC 604/604B will be attached to the retained copy of the SF 1034. The duplicate will be provided to the individual making the purchase.

(2) For checkage sales, the original initialed, signed, and receipted NAVMC 604/604B will be forwarded to the disbursing officer with form SF 1034. The duplicate NAVMC 604/604B will be filed in support of the retained copy of the form SF 1034. The triplicate NAVMC 604/604B will be given to the individual making the purchase.

e. Items which are not available for checkage sale will be lined out, entered on a new NAVMC 604/604B, and filed or returned to the individual's unit for future sale of backordered items.

f. Disposition of funds derived from the sale of individual uniform clothing to reservists will be processed per references (q) and (r) and local disbursing Standard Operating Procedures (SOP). Marine Corps Reserve units not directly supported by a disbursing office must transmit funds derived from the sale of individual uniform clothing by means of a postal money order. The unit will deduct the cost of the postal money-order fee from the gross amount of the proceeds of sales. A record of the transaction will be shown on the face of the SF 1034, per the following example:

                Total funds derived from sales $20.00
                Cost of postal money order   -1.25
                Total value of cash transmitted $18.75

g. Personnel of Marine Corps Reserve organizations located near a Military Clothing Sales Store (MCSS)/Retail Clothing Outlet (RCO) may make Marine Corps Forces Reserve funded or cash purchases only from the store on an as available basis (active duty personnel supported by the MCSS/RCO have priority of issue/sale). Reserve funded purchases must include the applicable Reserve MILPERS or Operations and Maintenance, Marine Corps Reserve (O&MMCR) appropriation data on the NAVMC 604/604B. Processing of NAVMC 604/604Bs for checkage sales for Reserve personnel will not be accomplished at an MCSS/RCO.

8006. ALTERATIONS AND ACCESSORIES. Reserve alterations will be provided utilizing Reserve Clothing Funds, per the guidelines provided in paragraph 2009.1 and figure 2-3 of this Manual. Units will contact the MFR Clothing Section for authorization prior to alterations being performed. SMCR units will provide a copy of the NAVMC 604/604B to the MFR Clothing Section. SMCR units will obtain blanket purchase agreements (BPAs) from reputable, local tailors that are able to accept Government credit cards. Upon completion of alterations by an authorized tailor, the SMCR unit must provide a copy of the alteration receipt/slip to the MFR Clothing Section. The MFR Clothing Section will make payment to the tailor.

8007. REPLACEMENT IN-KIND PROCESS. Replacement of unserviceable uniform items is authorized, on an item-for-item basis, to maintain the reservist's onhand clothing at the Reserve MRL quantities.

1. Requests from personnel for gratuitous replacement of clothing articles should be disapproved when the articles are missing and there is no satisfactory explanation for the loss, or the articles are unserviceable and have not been in the individual's possession long enough to become unserviceable through normal use. Replacement issues for articles avoidably lost or destroyed will be made by cash sale or checkage of the individual's pay account.

2. Individual clothing of enlisted personnel in the Marine Corps or Naval Reserve who receive clothing via the replacement in-kind

process may be replaced if such clothing has been lost, destroyed, damaged, or abandoned incident to their service provided:

    a. Such clothing was necessary or proper under attendant circumstances for the individual concerned.

    b. Such clothing was not in excess of the authorized allowance plus additional allowances, if presently entitled thereto. Unserviceable garments which are excess to authorized allowances will be recovered without replacement.

    c. Such clothing is obviously unserviceable and are being surrendered by the proper individual or that the replacement is on an otherwise authorized basis.

    d. The unit commander determines that there is no fault or negligence on the part of the individual.

8008. CLOTHING INSPECTIONS/INVENTORIES. Commanders of SMCR units shall hold annual clothing inspections/inventories, in addition to those inventories required per paragraph 3004 of this Manual. These inspections/inventories shall serve to determine whether the clothing in the possession of enlisted personnel is in serviceable condition and that the required quantity of clothing is possessed.

8009. TRANSFER BETWEEN SELECTED MARINE CORPS RESERVE (SMCR) UNITS, TO INDIVIDUAL READY RESERVE (IRR) STATUS, OR TO EXTENDED ACTIVE DUTY

1. The NAVMC 631/631A and duplicate copies of the NAVMC 604/604B will be inserted on top of the enlistment contract of the transferring individual's service record book (SRB) to ensure the gaining command is aware of any required subsequent issuance.

2. If unable to draw necessary replacement clothing, because of nonavailability prior to their transfer, a certificate listing the articles due the individual and signed by an officer authorized to approve such issues shall be placed in the individual's SRB. Upon joining a new organization, individuals shall be issued the items to which they are entitled.

3. <u>For those members transferring to another SMCR unit</u>. When enlisted personnel are transferred within the SMCR, the individuals will be allowed to retain the uniform clothing in their possession. The individual's new commander shall conduct an inventory of the clothing in the enlisted reservist's possession, per paragraph 3004 of this Manual. Discrepancies discovered by the inspection will be reconciled by issues/sales, as necessary, to complete the individual's clothing allowance. Any necessary replacement clothing that could not be provided at the previous unit and is documented by a nonavailablity certificate shall be issued at the new unit. The NAVMC 631/631A and duplicate copies of the NAVMC 604/604B shall be presented with the nonavailablity certificate at the time of the clothing issue.

4. <u>For those members transferred to IRR status</u>, the approved form shall be forwarded to the Commanding General, Marine Corps Reserve Support Command (CG, MCRSC) for inclusion in the individual's official military personnel file (OMPF).

5. <u>For those members being assigned to extended active duty</u> (more than 6 months of active duty), the SMCR activity commander will inventory the individual's clothing prior to transfer. The results of the inventory will be included, in ink, in the "on hand" column (<u>column 1</u>) and will be attested to on certificate No. 2 of the NAVMC 631/631A. The clothing record will then be forwarded to the individual's new activity commander. Upon reporting for active duty, a subsequent inventory will be conducted by the gaining commander and the reservist will be provided with quantities of clothing that comprise the difference between the amounts indicated in <u>column 1</u> as being on hand upon transfer and the quantities prescribed in the current MRL, per paragraph 9002 of this Manual. This issue will be posted to the "Return to Active Duty Issues" (<u>column 5</u>) and will likewise be attested to on certificate No. 3. A new NAVMC 631/631A will be prepared for those returning to reserve status following extended active duty, including those returning from combat per paragraph 9004 of this Manual. The new record will indicate in the "on hand" column (<u>column 1</u>) such quantities that comprise the present applicable allowances for personnel of the Marine Corps Reserve, inasmuch as the individual will have at least that amount of clothing on hand prior to separation from extended active duty.

8010. DOCUMENTATION AND DISPOSITION OF CLOTHING FORMS. As stated previously, all issues or replacements made via the Reserve replacement in-kind process will first be documented on a Combined Individual Clothing Requisition and Issue Slip (NAVMC 604/604B). Issues and recoveries shall then be recorded on the Individual Clothing Record (NAVMC 631/631A), as detailed below, and retained in the unit supply section. Both forms may be downloaded from the MCEFS, per paragraph 8005 preceding. Responsibility for the preparation and maintenance of clothing records rests directly with the unit commander. However, administrative responsibilities may be delegated to appropriate personnel. Care shall be exercised by all personnel having official access to the records to prevent unauthorized entries.

1. NAVMC 604/604B

    a. Entries to the NAVMC 631/631A will be made from the duplicate copy of the NAVMC 604/604B, when the amount of clothing authorized has been issued.

    b. After an initial issue has been recorded on the individual clothing record, the duplicate NAVMC 604/604B will be destroyed.

    c. When replacement issues to individuals are furnished with new or recovered clothing, the NAVMC 604/604B will be annotated "new clothing" or "recovered clothing" and the duplicate copy will be filed directly behind the individual clothing record. These slips will be destroyed when the person is transferred to the IRR or discharged from obligated Reserve service, whichever is earlier. The foregoing is necessary, since replacements of this type are not recorded in the NAVMC 631/631A inasmuch as they do not affect the amount of clothing on charge to the individual. The retention of the duplicate NAVMC 604/604B will help to ensure that the individual is not being provided an excessive amount of replacement clothing and will provide information for determination of clothing items to be recovered upon separation when items issued at government expense have been replaced via the replacement in-kind process.

2. NAVMC 631/631A

    a. A new NAVMC 631/631A will be established for personnel of the Marine Corps Reserve under the following conditions when:

(1) A person initially joins the Marine Corps Reserve.

(2) A reservist reenlists in the Marine Corps Reserve after the expiration of a prior enlistment.

(3) A reservist resumes or establishes an inactive duty status with the Marine Corps Reserve upon separation from the Regular Establishment after a period of initial active duty for training or a tour of extended active duty (more than 6 months of active duty).

(4) A reservist enlists in the Marine Corps Reserve as an initial active duty trainee.

(5) No recovery and reissue of clothing are necessary when a reservist reenlists immediately upon discharge. However, a new clothing record will be prepared and the "on hand" column (column 1) balance on the old form will be transferred to the new form. At this time, the clothing in the possession of an individual will be inspected and a determination will be made as to whether discrepancies will be resolved by replacement issues made in kind or whether the individual will be obliged to resolve such discrepancies by cash sale or checkage. Replacement issues will not be made to reservists until their reenlistment in the Marine Corps Reserve has been actually accomplished.

b. When a new NAVMC 631/631A has been established for personnel of the Marine Corps Reserve, the individual's old clothing record may be destroyed.

c. The NAVMC 631/631A is maintained and filed in the unit supply section. Upon an individual's transfer from one unit to another, the individual clothing record will be inserted on top of the enlistement contract in the transferring individual's SRB. Upon reporting in at the new unit, the individual's clothing record will be removed from the respective SRB and filed in the unit supply section.

d. Non-Required NAVMC 631/631A Postings. Issues which do not affect the total quantity of clothing on charge to a reservist shall not be posted to the NAVMC 631/631A. These include the following:

(1) Replacement issues made to replace like articles lost, worn out, or otherwise unserviceable which are replaced without charge on an item basis.

(2) Items furnished a reservist on a checkage or cash sale basis.

e. Entries to the "on hand" column (column 1) and the space provided for the date of the onhand entry will be made in pencil. This is to facilitate the changing of the data contained therein, as may be necessary by issue or recovery entries. However, the one exception in this regard occurs when the inspection of the individual's clothing is made prior to transfer to extended active duty (more than 6 months of active duty). At that time, the information under the "on hand" column and the date for the listed onhand figure will be made in ink. Entries in all other columns will be typewritten or made in ink.

f. Required NAVMC 631/631A Postings. Only transactions which affect the "on hand" or "balance" column of the NAVMC 631/631A will be posted. These include the following:

(1) Initial Issues.

(2) Issues that increase the balance of the articles on charge to the individual (such as supplementary allowance and special initial clothing allowance issues).

(3) Recoveries of articles for which no replacement is made.

g. Posting Reserve In-Kind Issues. Columns 2 and 3 have been reserved for recording issues made. Entries reflecting an issue will be made as follows:

(1) The amount furnished the reservist will be entered in the "issues" column (column 2 or 3).

(2) A pencil entry will be made in column 1 reflecting the new "on hand" balance. If a previous onhand figure appeared in the column, it will be erased and corrected according to the issue made.

(3) The date of the issue will be indicated in the space provided behind the word "issues" in the column.

(4) An entry will be made on Certificate 1 attesting to the issue described indicating information as follows:

(a) Date Made. Indicate the date of issue shown on the NAVMC 604/604B from which the posting is made.

(b) Organization Where Made. Indicate the organization shown on the NAVMC 604/604B as the issuing office.

(c) Issue Per Column. Indicate the number of the column to which the posting reflecting the issue was made.

(d) Attested To By. To be signed by the witnessing officer who verifies the preceding entries and destroys the form NAVMC 604 or 604b from which the entries are made.

(e) Date Attested. Indicate the date the preceding entries and attestation are made.

(5) The duplicate form NAVMC 604/604B from which the preceding entries are posted will be destroyed by the officer making the attestation, after the entries have been made and verified on the NAVMC 631/631A.

h. Posting Recoveries. Column 4 has been reserved for recording recoveries made. Entries reflecting a recovery will be made as follows:

(1) The amount recovered from the reservist will be entered in the "recovery" column (column 4).

(2) The date of the recovery will be indicated in the space provided behind the word "recovery" in the title.

(3) The entries made on certificate No. 1 apply, except that, in lieu of an issue, the recovery will be shown under the "recovery per" column item in the certificate.

i. Recording Inventories

(1) When an inventory of clothing is taken, such inventory should be verified against the "on hand" column (column 1).

(2) Normally, an inventory of an individual's clothing will not result in any quantitative entries on the NAVMC 631/631A. Discrepancies will be resolved by either a replacement in-kind, checkage, or cash sale, as appropriate. In any event, the quantity on charge to the individual would not be altered; hence, the "on hand" column (column 1) figure will remain unchanged.

(3) An inventory resulting in no quantitative changes in the figure in the "on hand" column (column 1) will be entered on the NAVMC 631/631A as follows:

(a) The date appearing in the "on hand" column (column 1) will be erased and the date of the inventory will be included in lieu thereof.

(b) The entries for Certificate No. 1 apply, except that, in lieu of an issue, the inventory will be attested to under the "on hand per" column item.

(c) In the event the inventory to be recorded represents a transfer inspection, the preceding instructions apply, except that, under the "on hand per" column, the word "transfer" will be written next to the "on hand" column designated.

8011. DISPOSITION OF RECOVERED AND/OR EXCESS CLOTHING

1. Recovered individual uniform clothing suitable for renovation will be renovated by laundering or drycleaning, as appropriate, and will be given priority of issue over new items to meet replacement requirements.

2. Recovered clothing will be handled per paragraph 6004 of this Manual.

8012. RETENTION PROCEDURES. Except as provided in paragraph 6003 preceding, enlisted personnel of the Marine Corps Reserve may retain all articles of individual uniform clothing in their possession upon separating from an SMCR unit.

8013. <u>ORGANIZATIONAL ISSUE OF DRESS BLUE UNIFORMS</u>. SMCR units
are authorized to stock and issue dress blue uniforms and other
uniform clothing for organizational issue, per paragraph 7005 of
this Manual. Historically, Marine Corps Reserve training centers
have maintained six dress blue uniforms (either male or female)
for use by all of the units located at the center. However,
there is no restriction on the quantity of uniform clothing items
provided via organizational issue as long as policy is maintained
per chapter 7 of this Manual.

INDIVIDUAL CLOTHING REGULATIONS

CHAPTER 9

DEPLOYMENT AND ACTIVATION/MOBILIZATION

INDIVIDUAL CLOTHING REGULATIONS

CHAPTER 9

DEPLOYMENT AND ACTIVATION/MOBILIZATION

9000. <u>INTRODUCTION</u>. This chapter provides policy and procedures for administration of clothing during deployments or service in combat.

9001. <u>SCOPE</u>. The instructions contained in this chapter apply to active duty Marines and Sailors serving with Marine Corps units (including those personnel activated/mobilized) during times of combat or under orders to proceed to combat areas or areas where emergent conditions exist. Except in time of war declared by the Congress, the terms "combat areas" and "areas where emergent conditions exist" as used in these instructions shall include areas where personnel are subject to hostile fire or explosion of hostile mines, or where they are on duty in an area in which they are in imminent danger of being exposed to hostile fire or explosion of hostile mines and in which, during the period they are on duty in that area, other members of the uniformed services are subject to hostile fire or explosion of hostile mines. Details on which organizations are responsible for issuance of uniform clothing to activated personnel are included in reference (dd).

9002. <u>MOBILIZED/ACTIVATED PERSONNEL</u>. Mobilized/activated personnel are divided into four categories for the issuance and/or replacement of uniform clothing:

- Activated enlisted reservists
- Activated Reserve Marine officers
- Other activated personnel
- Activated civilian support personnel

Instructions for each category are provided below.

1. <u>Activated Enlisted Reservists</u>. This category includes Selected Marine Corps Reserve (SMCR), Individual Mobilization Augmentee (IMA), and Individual Ready Reserve (IRR) "obligor" (see paragraph 2003.3 of this Manual) enlisted personnel.

a.   Commanders or mobilization support personnel will conduct a uniform clothing inventory, per paragraph 3005 of this Manual.

b.   Commanders will determine if fault or negligence is involved with deficient mandatory retention items, per paragraph 6002 of this Manual.

c.   Units will provide for clothing issues/replacement issues, per figure 2-2 of this Manual. See figure 3-1 of this Manual for the appropriate Functional Account Number (FAN) to use for these clothing issues/replacement issues and paragraph 3004 for proper issue/replacement documentation.

d.   Quantities of clothing issued will be the difference between the mandatory retention amounts indicated in the individual's clothing record (NAVCM 631/631A), per paragraph 6002 of this Manual, and the Minimum Combat Load (MCL) listed below. Replace any unserviceable clothing items, to include worn-out items or items that no longer fit properly due to weight or other physical changes occurring since release from active duty (SMCR and IMA reservists must maintain weight standards). Replaced clothing must be recovered.

<u>Minimum Combat Load (MCL)</u>

Item	Qty
Bag, Duffel	1
Belt, Web or Martial Arts	2
Boot, Combat TW or HW, pair	1
Buckle, for belt, web, khaki	2
Cap, Combat Utility, garrison, woodland or desert MARPAT (mission dependent)	1
Cap, Combat Utility, field, woodland or desert MARPAT (mission dependent)	1
Coat, Combat Utility, woodland or desert MARPAT (mission dependent) with name and service tapes	2
Socks, Boot	4
Trousers, Combat Utility, woodland or MARPAT (mission dependent) w/ name tape	2
Undershirt (for utility uniform)	6

e.   If activation orders state otherwise or the Gaining Force Commander (GFC) deems additional clothing is required, the activated reservist may be issued the difference between the mandatory retention amounts (NAVMC 631/631A) and the current MRL for personnel of the Regular establishment, per paragraph 2003.3 of this Manual.

   f. Activated Navy personnel may be issued the special initial clothing allowances, per paragraph 2004 of this Manual.

   g. If all required clothing is not available prior to transfer to the GFC, "due member" documentation is required per paragraph 3003 of this Manual.

   h. If required, supplementary clothing allowances authorized to the GFC may be issued to the activated reservist, per paragraph 2008 of this Manual. A Medium Dress Blue Supplementary Clothing Allowance is authorized for those personnel assigned to casualty assistance teams for funeral details.

   i. Commanders will initiate the Basic Clothing Replacement Allowance (BCRA) via unit diary entry to accrue commencing with the day following the completion of 6 months continuous active duty, without regard to time lost from the date of last authorization to the Initial Issue, per paragraph 2006 of this Manual.

   j. Upon demobilization, commanders must complete a clothing exit inventory and counseling per paragraph 3004 of this Manual.

2. Activated Reserve Marine Officers. Activated Reserve Marine officers will not receive clothing issues/replacement issues, but may be eligible for the Additional Active Duty Allowance if they remain on active duty beyond 90 days and it has been more than 2 years since they last served on active duty (for a period of more than 90 days), per paragraph 2007.4 of this Manual. Unit commanders must authorize this allowance and will initiate payment via unit diary entry.

3. Other Activated Personnel. This category includes recalled retirees, previously discharged personnel, and IRR "non-obligors" (see paragraph 2003 preceding). If within 90 days of discharge from all obligated service, the same procedures as listed in paragraph 9002.1 preceding will be followed. If beyond 90 days from discharge from all obligated service, retention of

uniform clothing is not required and a complete MCL or Initial Issue should be provided, as required, followed by steps (4) through (6) of paragraph 9002.1 preceding. The Initial Issue may be provided only once during 4 consecutive years and only once during any period of continuous active duty.

4. Activated Civilian Support Personnel. Civilian personnel activated to support the Marine Corps may be issued service or utility uniforms with no distinctive grade or Marine Corps or Navy device or insignia, per paragraph 2003.7 of this Manual.

9003. DEPLOYED BLOCKS. Combat Logistics Elements (CLEs) may draw clothing blocks from the supporting Military Clothing Sales Store (MCSS)/Retail Clothing Outlet (RCO) for deployments in excess of 60 days. Accounting, payment, and resupply procedures will be in accordance with the supporting MCSS/RCO Standard Operating Procedures (SOP).

9004. TRANSFERRING TO/FROM COMBAT

1. Storage Prior to Transfer to Combat. Units may set up a clothing control point for mass storage of individual uniform clothing items during deployment to a combat area, per the following procedures:

    a. Activity commanders operating clothing control points will be responsible for ensuring that stored clothing is properly documented on forms NAVMC 631/631A, per paragraph 3004 of this Manual.

    b. Only "issued" clothing will be documented on the NAVMC 631/631A; all other clothing will be considered "personal effects" and will be handled per reference(s).

    c. The clothing will be placed in an appropriate container, such as a fiberboard box, clothing bag, or duffel bag. The container will be secured following inventory and certification of NAVMC 631/631A, per paragraph 3004 of this Manual.

    d. A shipping tag or other locator identification card will be prepared indicating the name, grade, and SSN of the individual whose clothing is being stored. This tag or card will be securely attached to the container in which the clothing is stored. In addition, if a clothing or duffel bag is used to store clothing, the bag will bear identification markings, per reference (d).

    e. Clothing prepared for storage in the continental United States (INCONUS) will be forwarded to the Personal Effects and Baggage Center (PEBC), Marine Corps Base, Camp Lejeune or Camp Pendleton, as appropriate. Outside the continental United States (OCONUS), the clothing will be stored at the clothing control point until shipment to a PEBC is coordinated. In those cases when clothing is recovered for storage at areas other than the bases at which the PEBCs are located, supply officers will, prior to shipping such parcels, write to the officer in charge of the cognizant PEBC, advising of the number of such containers for storage and requesting shipping instructions.

    f. The subject clothing which is received by the PEBCs will be handled within those organizations per existing instructions.

    g. Activity commanders will ensure that the concerned PEBCs receive transfer rosters of personnel being returned from combat areas so that the stored clothing might be made available upon their return.

2. Replacement Issues Incident to Combat. For replacements required during combat, a personal property claim must be filed for applicable circumstances, per paragraph 2009.7 of this Manual. However, since timely replacement is essential for further combat operations, immediate replacements may be authorized locally, documented, and later reconciled with applicable personal property claims documents for vouchering. For those circumstances when a personal property claim is not applicable, the Major Subordinate Commander (MSC) commander is authorized to replace clothing for losses incident to combat.

    a. Replacement issues incident to combat include actual replacements during combat and replacement issues to hospitalized personnel and other personnel displaced from their clothing (to include prisoners, deserters, etc.) and for the burial of the dead, per paragraph 6005.1 and figure 3-1 of this Manual.

b. Minimum Traveling Uniform. The Minimum Traveling Uniform is a gratuitous health and comfort issue of uniform clothing necessary for the acceptable standards of personal appearance. Any portion of the Minimum Traveling Uniform, up to the total list provided in figure 9-1 following, may be issued as replacements incident to combat, as circumstances dictate. However, it is not necessary to issue the entire Minimum Traveling Uniform; only those items required for travel, based on the climate, environment, and destination will be furnished (i.e. conditions may not warrant the wear of the utility uniform).

c. All replacement issues must be documented on forms NAVMC 604/604B and NAVMC 631/631A per paragraphs 2000 and 3004 of this Manual, respectively. In the event that the individual's NAVMC 631/631A is not available, a copy of the NAVMC 604/604B will be mailed to the individual's command for proper documentation in the individual's official military personnel file (OMPF).

d. Combat replacement issues will be funded using MILPERS appropriations, which are controlled by HQMC vice the unit. FAN "72053" is used for these replacements, per figure 3-1 of this Manual.

e. Combat replacement issues must be approved by the unit's MSC commander.

3. Returning from Combat. Clothing inventories should be conducted as soon as feasible (i.e., upon arrival at clothing control point, during the return voyage, etc.), per paragraph 3004 of this Manual. Clothing which was kept in storage for the individual during a tour of duty in a combat area will be obtained and handled as follows:

a. Activities operating clothing control points will:

(1) Provide the following statement, if applicable:

"Form NAVMC 631/631A is/is not available. Form NAVMC 604/604B for gratuitous replacement of missing or damaged required uniform clothing was/was not issued."

(2) Authorize gratuitous replacement of any items damaged or lost during storage.

(3) If shipment of the clothing to the individual becomes necessary, it will be accomplished at Government expense and certificate No. 5B of the NAVMC 631/631A will be completed for this purpose.

(4) Maintain, for a period of 6 months, copies of form NAVMC 604/604B which were issued to combat returnees authorizing gratuitous replacement of missing or damaged uniform clothing and affect authorized replacements and document per paragraph 3004 of this Manual.

b. Commands joining combat returnees will:

(1) Compare clothing inventory with the individual's forms NAVMC 631/631A and NAVMC 604/604B.

(2) Affect authorized replacements and document per paragraph 3004 of this Manual.

(3) Assist the individual with processing a personal property claim, per paragraph 2009.7 of this Manual, for clothing items found to be missing through no fault or negligence by the individual.

c. Commands joining combat returnees who do not possess forms NAVMC 631/631A or 604/604B but have a statement from their previous unit stating they are authorized gratuitous replacement of required uniform clothing will:

(1) Query the clothing control point activity and/or the individual's former parent command to determine whether items were gratuitously issued.

(2) Affect authorized replacements and document per paragraph 3004 of this Manual.

(3) Assist the individual with processing a personal property claim, per paragraph 2009.7 of this Manual for missing items (i.e., those lost by the clothing control point or found to be missing through no fault or negligence by the individual).

9005. <u>SUSTAINMENT ISSUES OF ORGANIZATIONAL CLOTHING</u>.
Replacement issues of unserviceable organizationally issued
clothing may become necessary during combat. These replacement
issues are authorized as long as the handling procedures for
organizational clothing and equipment are followed, per chapter 7
of this Manual.

INDIVIDUAL CLOTHING REGULATIONS

Quantity		
Summer	Winter	Article
1	1	BELT, TROUSERS: web, khaki
1	1	BOOTS, MARINE CORPS COMBAT: hot or temperate weather, pair (as required)
1	1	BUCKLE: f/belt, web, khaki
1	1	BUCKLE: f/belt, coat
1	1	CAP, GARRISON, MAN'S: all-season, green
1	1	CAP, COMBAT UTILITY: field or garrison, woodland or desert MARPAT (as required)
1	1	CLASP, NECKTIE
1	1	COAT, MAN'S: all-weather
1	1	COAT, MAN'S: all-season, green, w/belt
1	1	COAT, COMBAT UTILITY: woodland or desert MARPAT w/ embroidered name and service tapes (as required)
3	3	DRAWERS, MAN'S: cotton, white, pair
0	1	GLOVES, LEATHER: black, pair
1	1	INSIGNIA, BRANCH OF SERVICE: garrison cap, black, screwpost
1	1	INSIGNIA, BRANCH OF SERVICE: service uniform collar, black, pair
2	2	INSIGNIA, GRADE, ENLISTED PERSONNEL: green on khaki (man's), pair
1	1	INSIGNIA, GRADE, ENLISTED PERSONNEL: green on scarlet, pair
1	1	INSIGNIA, GRADE, ENLISTED PERSONNEL: black, plastic, pair (3 pairs authorized if utilities are issued)
1	1	NECKTIE: khaki
1	2	SHIRT, MAN'S: polyester/wool, khaki, long-sleeve
1	0	SHIRT, MAN'S: polyester/wool, khaki, quarter-length-sleeve
1	1	SHOES, DRESS: black, pair
3	3	SOCKS: boot, pair
3	3	SOCKS: dress, black, pair
1	1	STRIPE, SERVICE: green on scarlet, pair
1	1	TROUSERS, MAN'S: all-season, green, pair
1	1	TROUSERS, COMBAT UTILITY: woodland or desert MARPAT w/ embroidered service tape (as required)
2	2	UNDERSHIRT: for utility uniform
2	2	UNDERSHIRT: white, for service uniform

Figure 9-1.--Minimum Traveling Uniform (Men's).

INDIVIDUAL CLOTHING REGULATIONS

Quantity Summer	Winter	Article
1	1	BELT, TROUSERS: web, khaki
1	1	BOOTS, MARINE CORPS COMBAT: hot or temperate weather, pair (as required)
1	1	BUCKLE: f/belt, web, khaki
1	1	CAP, GARRISON, WOMAN'S: all-season, green
1	1	CAP, COMBAT UTILITY: field or garrison, woodland or desert MARPAT (as required)
1	1	COAT, WOMAN'S: all-weather
1	1	COAT, WOMAN'S: all-season, green
1	1	COAT, COMBAT UTILITY: woodland or desert MARPAT w/ embroidered name and service tapes (as required)
0	1	GLOVES, LEATHER: black, pair
1	1	INSIGNIA, BRANCH OF SERVICE: garrison cap, black, screwpost
1	1	INSIGNIA, BRANCH OF SERVICE: service uniform collar, black, pair
2	2	INSIGNIA, GRADE, ENLISTED PERSONNEL: green on khaki (woman's), pair
1	1	INSIGNIA, GRADE, ENLISTED PERSONNEL: green on scarlet, pair
1	1	INSIGNIA, GRADE, ENLISTED PERSONNEL: black, plastic, pair (3 pairs authorized if utilities are issued)
1	1	NECK TAB, WOMAN'S: green
1	2	SHIRT, WOMAN'S: polyester/wool, khaki, long-sleeve
1	0	SHIRT, WOMAN'S: polyester/wool, khaki, short-sleeve
1	1	SHOES, DRESS, WOMAN'S: oxford, black, pair
1	1	SKIRT OR SLACKS, WOMAN'S: all-season, green (as required)
3	3	SOCKS: boot, pair
3	3	SOCKS: dress, black, pair
1	1	STRIPE, SERVICE: green on scarlet, pair
1	1	TROUSERS, COMBAT UTILITY: woodland or desert MARPAT w/ embroidered service tape (as required)
2	2	UNDERSHIRT: for utility uniform
2	2	UNDERSHIRT: white, for service uniform

Figure 9-2.--Minimum Traveling Uniform (Women's).

INDIVIDUAL CLOTHING REGULATIONS

APPENDIX A

ACRONYMS/ABBREVIATIONS

Acronym	Represents
AAFES	Army and Air Force Exchange Service
ACMC	Assistant Commandant of the Marine Corps
APF	Appropriated Funds
BCRA	Basic Clothing Replacement Allowance
BPA	Blanket Purchase Agreement
CDTS	Combat Development Tracking System
CID	Commercial Item Description
C&T	Clothing and Textiles
CMA	Clothing Monetary Allowance
CMC	Commandant of the Marine Corps
CG, MARCORLOGCOM	Commanding General, Marine Corps Logistics Command
CG, MARCORSYSCOM	Commanding General, Marine Corps Systems Command
CLE	Combat Logistics Element
CONUS	Continental United States
CRA	Clothing Replacement Allowance
CURR ACDU	Current Active Duty Date
DC	Deputy Commandant
DM	Due-Member
DoD	Department of Defense
DoDI	Department of Defense Instruction
DRMO	Defense Reutilization and Marketing Office
DRMS	Defense Reutilization and Marketing Service
DSCP	Defense Supply Center Philadelphia
DSSC	Direct Support Stock Control
DT	Dental Technician
FAN	Functional Account Number
FMS	Field Medical School
FY	Fiscal Year
HM	Hospitalman
HQMC	Headquarters Marine Corps
I&L	Installations and Logistics
ICR	Individual Clothing Regulations
IIP	Initial Issue Provisioning
INCONUS	Inside the Continental United States
IRR	Individual Ready Reserve

Acronym	Represents
JAGINST	Judge Advocate General Instruction
KYLOC	KY Logistics Operation Center
LOA	Line of Accounting
LPC	Logistics Capabilities Center
M&RA	Manpower and Reserve Affairs
MAID-P	Mobilization, Activation, Integration, and Deactivation Plan
MCAAT	Marine Corps Administrative Analysis Team
MCBul	Marine Corps Bulletin
MCCDC	Marine Corps Combat Development Command
MCCS	Marine Corps Community Services
MCEFS	Marine Corps Electronic Forms System
MCJROTC	Marine Corps Junior Reserve Officer Training Corps
MCL	Minimum Combat Load
MCO	Marine Corps Order
MCRD	Marine Corps Recruit Depot
MCRSC	Marine Corps Reserve Support Command
MCSS	Military Clothing Sales Store
MCTFSPRIM	Marine Corps Total Force Structure
MCUB	Marine Corps Uniform Board
MCX	Marine Corps Community Services Exchange
MOA	Memorandum of Agreement
MOS	Military Occupational Specialty
MOBCOM	Mobilization Command
MILPERS	Military Personnel Marine Corps
MRL	Minimum Requirements List
MSG Bn	Marine Corps Security Guard Battalion
NAF	Nonappropriated Funds
NEXCOM	Navy Exchange Command
NROTC	Naval Reserve Officer Training Corps
NWCF	Navy Working Capital Fund
OCC	Officer Candidates Class
OCONUS	Outside Continental United States
OCS	Officer Candidate School
OLA	Office of Legislative Affairs
OQR	Officer Qualification Record
O&MMC	Operations and Maintenance Marine Corps
P&R	Programs and Resources
PLC	Platoon Leaders Class
PM-ICE	Program Manager, Infantry Combat Equipment

Acronym	Represents
PMCUB	Permanent Marine Corps Uniform Board
SDN	Standard Document Number
POM	Program Objective Memorandum
PQDR	Product Quality Deficiency Report
QA	Quality Assurance
QDR	Quality Deficiency Report
R&D	Research and Development
RCO	Retail Clothing Outlet
RP	Religious Person
SCRA	Standard Clothing Replacement Allowance
SDR	Supply Discrepancy Report
SICA	Secondary Inventory Control Activity
SIUUA	Special Initial Utility Uniform Allowance
SISUA	Special Initial Service Uniform Allowance
SMCR	Selected Marine Corps Reserve
SRB	Service Record Book
SRP	Supply Request Package
SSN	Social Security Number
TAC	Tactical Address Code
TAD	Temporary Additional Duty
T/E	Table of Equipment
T/O	Table of Organization
UCDPP	Uniform Clothing Deferred Payment Plan
UNS	Universal Needs Statement

APPENDIX B

INDEX

Item/Subject	Paragraph(s)
Burial of the Dead	2009, 3004, Figure 3-1, 6005, 9004
Cash Clothing Allowances	0002, 1002, 1006, 2007, 3003
Cash Allowances for Officers	2007, 3003
Civilian Clothing Monetary Allowances	See "Civilian Clothing Allowances"
Miscellaneous Enlisted Cash Clothing Allowances	2007, 3003
Personal Items Allowance for Enlisted Women	2007, 3003
Replacement Allowances	See "Replacement Allowances"
Cash Sales	
Regular	5003, 6002
Reserve	5003, 6002, 8004, 8005
Store	See "Retail Clothing Outlet (RCO)"
Catalog Action Requests (form DD 1277)	1007-1008
Central Stocking for Clothing	5003, 7005
Checkage Sales	
Regular	2009, 5004
Reserve	2009, 5004, 8005, 8007, 8010
Civilians	See "Activated Personnel"
Civilian Clothing Allowances	2007, Figure 2-1
Civilian Clothing Replacement Allowance	
Conditions of Entitlement	
Initial Permanent Duty Civilian Clothing Allowance	
Requests for Civilian Clothing Allowances	
TAD Civilian Clothing Allowance	
Class II Individual Combat Clothing & Equipment (ICCE)	See "Organizational Clothing and Equipment"
Clothing Allowance	
Budget	1003-1006, 1008-1009
Cash Clothing Allowances	See "Cash Clothing Allowances"
Clothing Replacement Allowance (CRA)	See "Clothing Replacement Allowance"
Fielding	1003-1006, 1008, Figures 1-1 and 1-2, 6004
Implementation	1003-1006, Figure 1-2
Initial Clothing Allowances	See "Initial Clothing Allowances"
Initial Clothing Allowance Issue to Officer Programs	2005
Miscellaneous Clothing Allowances	2007-2008, 3004, Figure 3-1, 6005
Replacement	See "Replacement Allowances"
Requests	See "Clothing Requests"

INDIVIDUAL CLOTHING REGULATIONS

INDIVIDUAL CLOTHING REGULATIONS

Item/Subject	Paragraph(s)
Fit, Clothing	0002, 1002, 1008, 2009, Figure 2-3, 3005, 5004, 6005, 9002
Forms, Clothing	
Catalog Action Requests (DD 1277)	1007-1008
Combined Individual Requisition and Issue Slip (NAVMC 604/604B)	See "NAVMC 604/604B"
Due-Member (DM)	3003
Individual Clothing Record (NAVMC 631/631A)	See "NAVMC 631/631B"
Personal Property Claims	2009
Product Quality Deficiency Report (PQDR)	See "PQDR"
Standard Form (SF 1034)	3003, 5004, 8005
Standard Form (SF 368)	See "PQDR"
Supply Discrepancy Report (SDR)	1007, 5004
Transmittal of Clothing Issue Slips (NAVMC 604A)	3003, 5004, 8005
Funding	
APF	5005
HQMC	2009, 3002
MILPERS	2009, Figure 2-3, 3002
NAF	5005
O&MMC	See "Operations and Maintenance, Marine Corps"
Unit/Organization	See "Operations and Maintenance, Marine Corps"
Functional Account Number (FAN)	2009, 3002, 3003, Figure 3-1, 5004, 6005, 8005, 9002, 9003
Report	3002
FY Allowances	0002, 2003
Health and Comfort Issue	See "Minimum Traveling Uniform"
Honor Graduate	2009
Hospitalized Personnel	2009, 3004, Figure 3-1, 9004
HQMC Funding	See "Funding"
Individual Combat Clothing & Equipment (ICCE)	See "Organizational Clothing and Equipment"
Individual Ready Reserve (IRR)	2003, 6002, 8003, 8009, 8010, 9002
Initial Clothing Allowances	1009, 2003
Activated Personnel	See "Activated Personnel"
Enlisted Musicians	2003, Figure 3-1
Initial Permanent Duty Civilian Clothing	2007, Figure 2-1
Officer Programs	1009, 2003, 2005, 3003, Figure 3-1, 6002
Officers	2003, 2004, 2007, Figure 3-1
Recruits	2000-2003
Reduced Initial	2003
Reenlistees	2003
Reserve Reenlistees	2003
Seabag Review	1004

INDIVIDUAL CLOTHING REGULATIONS

INDIVIDUAL CLOTHING REGULATIONS

Item/Subject	Paragraph(s)
Officer	
Clothing Allowances	2009
Commissioned Officers	See "Cash Clothing Allowances"
Programs/Training Issues	1009, 2003, 2005, 2007, 3003, 3005, Figure 3-1, 6002, 6005
Warrant Officers	See "Cash Clothing Allowances"
Officer Candidate Class (OCC)	See "Officer Candidate School (OCS)"
Officer Candidate School (OCS)	
Clothing Replacement	6005
Navy ROTC	2005, 2007
Officer Candidates Class (OCC)	1009, 2005, 3003, 3005, Figure 3-1, 6002, 6005
Platoon Leaders Class (PLC)	1009, 2005, 3003, 3005, Figure 3-1, 6002, 6005
Service Academy	2005
Officer Programs	See "Officer Candidate School"
Official Military Personnel File (OMPF)	2009, 3003, 3004, 5004, 6002, 6005, 8009, 9004
Operations and Maintenance, Marine Corps (O&MMC)	2008, 2009, Figure 2-3, 3002, 3003, 5003, 5005, 6005, 7002, 7004, 7005
Operations and Maintenance, Marine Corps Reserve (O&MMCR)	8005
Optional Clothing Items	1008, 4003, 5002, 5003, 5005
Organizational Clothing and Equipment	
Accounting	3004, 7005
Class II Individual Combat Clothing & Equipment (ICCE)	5005, 7002, 7003
Funding	Figure 2-3, 7002
Laundering	7005
Marking	7004
NBCDE	7003
Personal Retention Items	7003
Recovery	7005
Requisitioning	Figure 2-3, 5005, 7005
Reserves	8013
Sustainment	9005
TAM Type 3 Items	7003
Types	7002, 7003
Uniform Clothing	2008, Figure 2-3, 7003, 8013
Permanent Marine Corps Uniform Board (PMCUB)	1000, 1004, 2007, 2008
Personal Effects	2003, 3004, 6003, 9000
Personal Items	2000, 2007, 3003, 5002
Personal Items Allowance for Enlisted Women	2007, 3003

B-8

INDIVIDUAL CLOTHING REGULATIONS

Item/Subject	Paragraph(s)
Personal Property Claims	
Authorized Claims	2009, Figures 2-3, 2-4 and 3-1, 9004
Forms Distribution	2009, 9004
How to Submit	2009, 9004
Non-Authorized Claims	2009
Processing	2009, 9004
Personal Retention Items	3004, 7003
Phase-in/out Plan	0002, 1008, 2006, 5005
Platoon Leaders Class (PLC)	See "Officer Candidate School (OCS)"
Pricing	1003
Non-System (Commercial)	5002, 5003
Supply System	2006, 2009, 5002, 5005
Prisoners	See "Miscellaneous Issues"
Product Quality Deficiency Report (PQDR)(SF 368)	0002, 1004-1008, 5004, 6005
Profile Changes	
Initial Training	2009, Figures 2-3 and 3-1, 3005
Medical	6005
Program Objective Memorandum (POM)	1004, 1006, 1008, Figure 1-1
Programs and Resources (P&R), Responsibilities	1005
Quality Deficiency Report (QDR)	5004
Rates, Clothing Allowance	1003, Figure 1-1, See also "MCBul 10120"
Records Management	2009, 3003, 3004
MCSS	See "Military Clothing Sales Store"
Reserve	8002, 8010
Sources of Supply	5003
Recovered Clothing	1002, 1006, 1009, 2005, 2008-2009, Figure 2-3, 6000, 6002-6005, 7003, 8003, 8005, 8010, 8011, 9002
Recovered Clothing Sales	2009, 5005, 6004, 6005
Recruit Incentive Issues	2009
Recruit Training Issues	See "Initial Clothing Allowances"
Recruit Training Replacements	6005
Reduced Initial Allowances	2003, Figure 3-1
Activated Personnel	
Enlisted Prisoners	
Officers and Warrant Officers	
Reserve Reenlistees	
Unsuccessful Officer Candidates	
Repairs, Uniform	2009, 5004

INDIVIDUAL CLOTHING REGULATIONS